Derek Robinson

Rugby: success starts here

Illustrated by John Gully

Pan Books London and Sydney

First published 1969 by Pelham Books Ltd
This revised edition published 1975 by Pan Books Ltd,
Cavaye Place, London SW10 9PG
ISBN 0 330 24168 0
© Derek Robinson 1969, 1975

Printed in Great Britain by
Richard Clay (The Chaucer Press) Ltd, Bungay, Suffolk

Rugby: success starts here

Derek Robinson was born in 1932. After National Service in the RAF – spent claustrophobically in underground ops rooms – he went up to Cambridge on a State Scholarship and read History. He planned to be a journalist but the money looked grim so he went into advertising instead – five years in London, six in New York, working on everything from bulldozers and whisky to oil companies and the *Wall Street Journal*. In 1967 he chucked it up and lived in Portugal for a year, then returned via the Channel Isles to England where he and his American wife now live. He is the author of the acclaimed *Goshawk Squadron*, also published in Pan. Apart from fiction, he has contributed to *Punch* and the *Guardian*; broadcasts regularly on sport; writes a weekly newspaper column; and has compiled a bestselling guide to Westcountry dialect, *Krek Waiter's Peak Bristle*.

This book covers all changes to the laws of Rugby up to and including those made in 1975

Contents

Illustrations

I should like to thank Peter Brook
and Don Rutherford for their great help
in the preparation of this book

D.R.

Introduction

There is no secret about how to play Rugby, any more than there is a secret about how to play basketball, or tennis, or stud poker. The laws of the game are written down for all to see. There may be a lot of secrets about how to *win*, but there is no secret about how to play.

Moreover, it's pretty obvious that a player should learn how to play a game before he starts thinking about how to win. Any poker player who got into a game without knowing whether a full house beats a flush, or *vice versa*, would have a pretty unhappy time of it.

And yet it is a fact that tens of thousands of Rugby players do not fully understand the laws of their game. What's more, these players have given up hope of ever knowing all the laws. They were never properly taught them when they began playing, and they don't intend to start learning them now.

As a result, tens of thousands of players are playing well below their true capacity. Simply because they don't completely understand what is allowed and what is prohibited, they can never be sure that they're making the most of the first, and steering clear of the second.

This has nothing to do with a player's physical fitness, or experience, or natural ability. It makes no difference whether a man is playing for a first-class club or a village 2nd XV – either he understands a particular law, or he doesn't. And if he doesn't, then he must be handicapped when playing against opponents who do, even if they're less fit, less experienced or less gifted than he is. That, too, is pretty obvious.

When a player tries to play Rugby without fully understanding the laws of the game three things happen.

The first is that he makes stupid mistakes which give his opponents opportunities to score. These mistakes are the result of *active* ignorance – ignorance which gets a player into trouble.

Take the law of off-side, for instance. This is something of a mystery to many players (perhaps to most). A man who doesn't realize that he is in an off-side position is liable to charge into the game and risk giving away a penalty kick. On the other hand, if he's not sure whether he's *on*-side, he's likely to do nothing at all. This is exactly what the other team would like him to do.

Furthermore, his ignorance makes him increasingly unsure. Suppose he gets penalized for off-side play. He still doesn't know exactly what it was that he did wrong, or how to avoid doing it again. All he knows is that the enemy is taking a shot at goal, and it's his fault. So in future he hangs back, for fear of making a mistake – a mistake which he can't really describe even to himself.

In these days of siege-gun kickers, when penalty goals decide the outcome of many matches, indescribable mistakes are something no team can afford.

The second thing that happens to a player who doesn't fully understand the laws is that he fails to grab his chances. Often this does not involve the referee at all. The referee applies those laws which lay down what the players *must* or *must not* do – but there are plenty of laws in Rugby which tell him what he *may* do if he wants to. If a player doesn't claim his privileges the game won't break down; but a good attacking opportunity will go begging. This is the effect of *passive* ignorance – ignorance of the freedom which the laws allow.

A good example is the advantage law. A player who doesn't know how this works will never be ready to seize on his opponents' mistakes and exploit them. His failure is not that he is breaking any laws, but that he isn't *using* them properly.

And the laws are there to be used. They are not a set of iron commandments; they are a description of the game. It's a positive, creative game, and the purpose of the laws is positive and creative.

The third thing which happens to a player who doesn't fully understand the laws is that he often picks up a lot of half-baked half-truths, and adds them to his game. This is *cock-eyed* ignorance.

One of the most cock-eyed of these half-truths is the myth that a player must not pass the ball when he is lying on the ground *under any circumstances*. Many players – perhaps an actual majority – believe this. They have never looked in the laws to see if it's true, but they faithfully carry it out. Once more, their ignorance is holding them back. Cock-eyed ideas about the laws may not be illegal, but they certainly weaken the game.

It's an extraordinary situation when so many players are resigned to going through their playing careers without fully understanding what they're doing. And yet it's true. In no other sport are the players so vague about the laws of the game. Yet the laws of Rugby are not much more difficult than those of other games. Indeed, Rugby is based on one very simple idea: the idea that each player should be as free as possible to get the ball and help his side score with it.

That obviously cuts out any interference with a player who hasn't got the ball. It lets everybody concentrate on the man who *has* got it. And it means that any number of players may handle, kick or pass the ball, one after another, keeping the game going continuously.

When you know the basic principles behind Rugby, the laws become quite straightforward. Rugby is meant to be fast-moving and continuous, with as few stoppages as possible, so the laws are against things like deliberately lying on the ball, or refusing to let go of it when you're tackled. The aim is *positive* – to keep the game going and the ball moving, and let everyone get on with it.

The idea behind scrums and line-outs is simply to re-start the game, quickly and fairly, once it's stopped.

The purpose of the off-side law is simply to keep each team more or less intact. A man is off-side when he's in front of a player on his own team who has the ball or who last played it, and for the moment he's out of the game. It's as simple as that. Without off-side the game would become so scattered and confused that, like the retreat from Moscow, you couldn't see the action for the players. Off-side makes the difference between an all-for-one and a free-for-all.

The law against throwing the ball forward makes sense once you understand off-side. If you give a forward pass, the man who takes it must be in front of you – and so off-side.

And if you mustn't throw it forward, you obviously shouldn't *knock* it forward, either; hence the law against the knock-on.

These laws are both simple and useful. If you abolished off-side, allowed forward passes and ignored knock-ons, the result wouldn't be better Rugby; it would be a kind of sloppy handball.

The need for laws about scoring, kicking and the in-goal (where scoring takes place) is pretty obvious.

Finally, there is the advantage law, which can trump nearly all the rest. This simply allows the referee to let play continue when one team breaks a law and their opponents take advantage of this. The advantage law covers ninety-nine per cent of all Rugby.

True Rugby can be played only if the players know the laws and honestly try to follow them. Accidentally breaking a law is bad luck; deliberately doing so is trying to distort the whole shape of the game. It's cheating in its most childish form, because in the long run the player is only cheating himself. It's the players who benefit from the laws, so it's up to the players to apply them.

That's why there's only one referee for thirty players. If everyone uses the laws, and doesn't abuse them, one referee is all you need.

The better you know the laws, the more you'll enjoy the game. And if the French, Italians, Poles, Japanese, Rumanians, Portuguese, Fijians and God-knows-who-else can master them, so can you. There is no secret about Rugby, but before you start thinking about how to win games, you should make sure you know what the game itself is all about. Winning Rugby starts here.

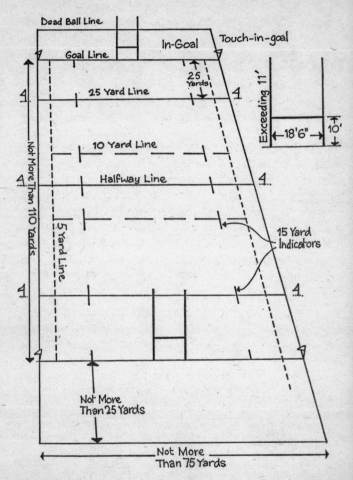

The playing area

Now that Rugby has gone metric, 110 yards equal 100 metres, 75 yards equal 69 metres and 25 yards equal 22 metres. For smaller distances the figures remain the same; thus 5, 10 and 15 yards become 5, 10 and 15 metres. This applies throughout the laws of the game. Goal dimensions are: crossbar 3 metres high, 5·6 metres long; uprights exceeding 3·4 metres.

One Off-side in open play

Not at scrums, rucks, mauls or line-outs

'More players have nervous breakdowns trying to understand the off-side law,' a research expert recently reported,
'than get kicked to death by green canaries.'

Which is a pity, because off-side is basically simple. In
open play, you are off-side when you are in front of a player
of your own team who has the ball, or who last played it.
And you must not take part in the game in any way until
you become on-side again.

This means much more than not touching the ball or the
man who has the ball.

Figure 1 What puts a player in an off-side position – being in
front of a player of his own team who either has the ball (*left*), or
who last played the ball (*right*)

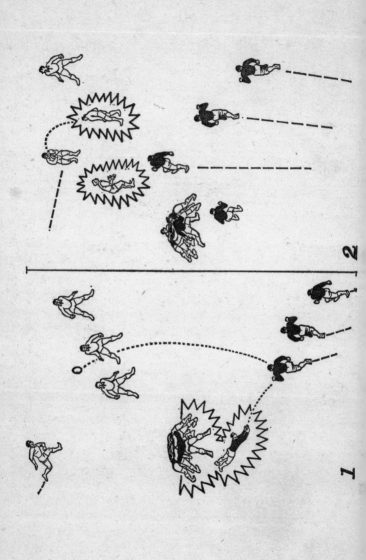

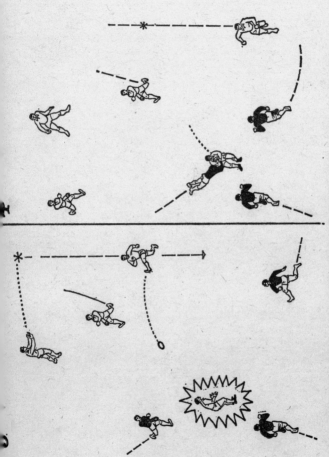

Figure 2 Typical piece of play, demonstrating off-side and on-side positions. Players marked with a starburst are in an off-side position. *See* description on next page

It means you must not even *go near* the ball. It means you must keep out of the way of the man who has it, of anybody he might intend to pass to, and of anybody who might try to tackle him. When you are off-side you must do nothing to influence the course of the game. Temporarily, you are on ice.

Take comfort. There is nothing to be ashamed, disgusted or suicidal about in being off-side. Everybody is off-side at some time or other. You get into trouble only when you try to take part in the game before you have been put properly on-side.

How off-side and on-side work (see examples on pp 18–19)

1 From a scrum, the ball goes to the Blue stand-off, who kicks ahead. All the Blue forwards and the Blue scrum-half are off-side. Everyone else is on-side.

2 The White full-back catches the ball. All the White players in front of him are off-side. The Blue stand-off follows up his kick, passing the Blue forwards and scrum-half and putting them on-side.

3 The White full-back passes to his wing-threequarter, who gains ground, thus putting some White players on-side, and cross-kicks.

4 The White wing-threequarter keeps on running, thus passing the remaining White players and putting them on-side – including the White player who now catches the cross-kick. A Blue player, running back from the White half, tackles him. This Blue player is in front of the ball but not off-side. *See* Figure 2.

What good does off-side do?

It is not hard to see the reason for the off-side law, once you see the mess we'd be in without it. If players could station themselves anywhere in the field, no matter where play was, you would have some of them camping permanently on their opponents' goal-line, just waiting for the ball to be booted their way. Players would be scattered everywhere, and both sides would constantly kick ahead in the hope of reaching someone and getting an easy score. Rugby would be basketball or, worse still, soccer.

As it is, off-side does not paralyse a player; it just keeps him quiet (off-the-side) until he has been put on-side and has thus rejoined the team (on-the-side).

Always remember:
Being off-side is not a matter of being in front of the ball! In open play, you are off-side only when you're in front of someone *on your team* who has the ball, or who last played it.

On-side in open play
(not at scrums, rucks, mauls or line-outs)
On-side means you are not off-side (obviously), so you can take part in the game again.

There are *seven ways* of getting yourself on-side. *See* Figure 3.

Four depend on what your own team does:
1 A team-mate, carrying the ball, runs in front of you.
2 A team-mate who kicked the ball when behind you now runs in front of you.
3 Any other team-mate who was on-side when the ball was kicked now runs in front of you.
4 You run behind any of these team-mates.

The other three depend on what your opponents do:
5 An opponent runs five yards with the ball.
6 An opponent plays the ball – kicks it, passes it, or just plain drops it.
7 An opponent *intentionally* touches the ball but does not catch it.

On-side balances off-side. The laws try to discourage you from getting off-side by making you do a little penance before they let you back into the game. You have to return

Figure 3 Seven ways an off-side player can be put on-side – but note that the last three (D, E, F) do not put him on-side if he is within ten yards of an opponent waiting to receive the ball

(A) Team-mate with ball runs ahead

(B) Team-mate kicks, runs ahead, or another on-side team-mate runs ahead

(C) Off-side player runs behind ball-carrier

RUNS 5 YDS.

(D) Opponent runs five yards with ball

(E) Opponent passes or kicks

(F) Opponent intentionally
touches ball
See p 21

to your team, or wait until your team (in the shape of an on-side player) comes up and joins you.

Note that, in a kick-ahead situation, you can be put on-side by any other player on your team who was on-side when the ball was kicked. So even if the kicker is brought down as he makes his kick, and is unable to follow it up, any player level with him or behind him can run forward and put his team-mates on-side.

In short, you can be put on-side by any player who is himself on-side when the ball is kicked.

But *until* you're put on-side, you must keep out of the game and give your opponents room for one free go – a chance to start something without fear of interruption from you. Only when one of them has run five yards with the ball, or passed it, or kicked it, or done *something*, can you come out of your trance and join in the action again.

And sometimes you cannot even do that, as we shall now reveal.

The 'ten-yard' off-side law

If you're off-side and less than ten yards from an opponent who is waiting to catch the ball, there's only one thing to do: get the hell out of it. This situation usually arises when a team-mate behind you kicks the ball ahead, and an opponent is waiting for it to come down.

Nothing your opponents or your team may do can help you here. You must *immediately* remove yourself ten yards from the opponent who is waiting for the ball, and fast, too.

Figure 4 The 'Ten-Yard' Law. An off-side player must not stay within ten yards of an opponent waiting to catch the ball, and until he has removed himself, no action by an opponent can put him on-side

If things are moving so rapidly that you cannot *avoid* being less than ten yards from the opponent when he catches the ball, then just beat it as smartly as you can, and the referee won't say anything.

It's worth repeating. When you are off-side under the 'Ten-Yard' law there is only one thing to do: immediately and quickly retire ten yards from the waiting opponent. It's worth repeating because what you *must* do is not what you *want* to do. Here is an opponent waiting to catch the ball, and here you are near enough to close in and clobber him; naturally you don't want to run away. It's a strange and unnatural reaction. But it's what the law says you must do, and do at once. This is the only occasion in the game of Rugby when the ball is in open play and you are required to run *away from* the action. The habit does not come easily. You just have to work at it.

On-side under the 'Ten-Yard' law
Retiring ten yards does not, of course, automatically put you on-side and therefore back in the game. All it does is

Figure 5 The 'Ten-Yard' Law. Once an off-side player has obeyed the 'Ten-Yard' law, he can rejoin the game as soon as he's been put on-side – either by a team-mate or by an opponent

keep you out of trouble. If you don't retire ten yards you are *criminally* off-side, and liable to be penalized. After you've retired ten yards you may still be off-side, depending on what else has happened in the game, but at least you are safe.

While you *are* retiring ten yards, the only way you can become on-side is through your own efforts or the efforts of your team-mate who last kicked the ball: either you can run behind him or he can run in front of you; it adds up to the same thing. So if he follows up fast enough, you might not need to cover the full ten yards.

Suppose, for instance, that you are in front of your full-back when he puts up a high kick ahead. You discover that you are only a few feet from an opponent who is getting ready to catch the ball, so you immediately turn and run. Meanwhile, your full-back has been hotly pursuing his kick, and before you've had time to cover more than about five yards, he passes you. This puts you on-side; you can stop beating it and join in the game again.

Once you *have* retired the full ten yards, you're in the same position as any other off-side player, so you can be put on-side by your opponents as well as by your team-mate. If one of them runs five yards with the ball, or kicks or passes or drops it, or intentionally touches it, you can go straight back into the game. But *until* you've retired your ten yards, nothing your opponents do can put you on-side. Nothing.

The reason why. The 'Ten-Yard' law makes sense. As an off-side player you must not take any part in the game; and your opponent cannot be expected to concentrate on catching a greasy ball coming out of the sun if you're standing right next to him, breathing hard. Of course, *you* know you are off-side, so *you* know that you are not going to lay a finger on him. But *he* doesn't know that, and your magnetic presence might make him nervous. Or you might accidentally get in his way. Or simply not get *out* of his way. So the law says you *must* get out of his way *before* he gets the ball – and keep on getting out of it until you're ten yards off.

Two rules to remember

1 If you are off-side and less than ten yards from an opponent waiting to catch the ball, you can never be put on-side

by any action of your opponents, so don't wait for it. Don't wait for anything. Clear off.

2 Any *other* time you are off-side in open play, you are *always* put on-side the moment an opponent kicks, passes or deliberately touches the ball – so look out for that.*

The penalty for off-side

There are, in fact, *two* penalties for off-side play, and the other side can choose which one it wants.

You will remember (how could you ever forget?) that you are penalized for off-side when you are in front of a player on your own team who has the ball or last played it, and you try to take part in the game.

Now the penalty – and pay attention, because this isn't as easy as the rest – the penalty can be *either* a penalty kick where you (the off-side player) took part in the game *or* a scrum where he (your team-mate) last played the ball.

Remember that it takes two to make off-side – you, and your mate who had the ball behind you – and the penalty is either a kick where you are now, or a scrum where he was then.

If this all sounds a bit overdone, believe me that it makes good sense in practice, and it's worth understanding, because one day you might be captain of a team when an opponent gets pinched for being off-side and the referee will look you straight in the eyes and say: 'Kick or scrum?' And if you stand on one leg and say you haven't the faintest idea, the ref is going to give you a very old-fashioned look and the selectors are going to give you a very modern rocket.

Here are two examples which show you how the kick-here-or-scrum-there penalty works out. Blues are playing Whites.

---

* But see chapter 6.

Figure 6 Penalty for off-side play. The White team gets a choice of a penalty kick or a scrum. Here they would probably take the kick

1 From a scrum on the Whites' 25-yard line, Blues win the ball, which goes to the Blue fly-half. He grub-kicks ahead and a Blue forward who is in front of him (and therefore off-side) plays the ball. Now Whites can *either* take a penalty kick where the Blue forward went wrong *or* a scrum at the place where the Blue fly-half kicked ahead. Since the scrum would give them only a few extra yards, and since they are defending, they probably choose the penalty kick. *See* Figure 6.

2 Near his own goal-line, the Blues' full-back kicks for touch, misses, and the ball goes to a White player. A Blue player less than ten yards from him makes no effort to retire,

Figure 7 Penalty for off-side play. Here the White team would probably prefer the scrum to the penalty kick

and so is penalized for off-side under the 'Ten-Yard' law. Whites can take *either* a penalty kick where the off-side Blue player was standing *or* a scrum where the Blue full-back kicked. The penalty kick would be in mid-field, perhaps too far out for Whites to kick a goal, but the scrum would be near their opponents' goal-line; so Whites probably choose the scrum. *See* Figure 7.

Accidental off-side

What happens to a player who is off-side, who is really sincerely making every effort not to interfere with the game, but who, despite himself, gets involved in it? (For instance, when a team-mate who has the ball bumps into him.)

You will be relieved to hear that the laws treat him with dignity and restraint. Provided the referee is satisfied that the team in possession gained no advantage from the accidental off-side, he lets play go on. If, on the other hand, he considers that it has improved their chances, he orders a scrum, with their opponents putting the ball in.

Two The tackle

One of the big things about Rugby, as we never tire of repeating, is that it should be fast-moving and continuous, with as few stoppages as possible.

On the other hand, the big thing about the tackle is that it latches on to something that is moving fast and stops it dead, or slightly stunned.

Clearly, tackles must be made; but then the game must go on. That is what the law of the tackle tries to bring about. This, too, is quite simple, as long as you know *what is a tackle and what is not.*

'A tackle' in the laws is not always the same as what you or I, in our slack and slovenly way, would call a tackle. We

Figure 8 *This is not a tackle*, as the laws define it, because although the player is brought down and held, the ball has not touched the ground and he can still play it. Nevertheless, because he is lying on the ground with the ball, he must *immediately* do something with it: play it, or release it and roll away from it

see one herbert with a grim expression fling himself at another herbert with the ball and a grim expression and, by annexing the second herbert's ankles, cut him down like some proud monarch of the forests; and we say to each other, 'Not a bad tackle, that. Bit high.' But in actual fact, according to the law, the second herbert hasn't necessarily been tackled at all. Brought down, yes; humbled, muddied

Figure 9 *This is not a tackle* either, according to the laws. The player is held and cannot run – but he is still able to pass the ball, and therefore free to do so

and severely jolted even unto the third and fourth back teeth, yes; but tackled – not necessarily. There is a big difference between 'tackled' and 'brought down'.

The law says a player is tackled when he has got the ball and an opponent has got *him*, so that *either* he cannot play the ball *or* the ball touches the ground. And it says that he *must* then let go of the ball *at once*.

So that is what has to happen before you can say you've legally tackled a player: you must hold him in the field-of-

Figure 10 *This is a tackle*, even though the player has not been brought down. He is held, and because his arms are pinned he can't pass the ball, so he must drop it

play in such a way that he cannot get free and he cannot play the ball (except by releasing it). Or alternatively, you must hold him in the field-of-play so that the ball touches the ground. Do either of these and he must let go of the ball. So you have won.

Don't do it, of course, and he need not let go of the ball, so you haven't won. That's why you should learn the difference between being tackled and being brought down.

On every Rugby clubhouse wall there should be stencilled in foot-high letters of scarlet the following manifesto:

You have not been tackled unless you are held and the ball touches the ground, or unless he gets such a vice-like grip around you that you can't get free and you can't do anything with the ball except drop it, which is what you must do pronto or face the music.

Might take up a bit of space, but it would be worth it if people stopped that sheep-like bleating of 'Passing off the

Figure 11 *This is a tackle*, because the player is held and the ball has touched the ground. He must let go of it, and not touch it again until he's on his feet

ground!' you hear so much. There is nothing wrong with passing off the ground: nothing. If an opponent tries to tackle you and doesn't quite make it but you fall over, you can pass the ball off the ground. Why not? Or you can leap up and make off with it.

If he tries to tackle you again and makes a better job of it – practice tells, you see – but you manage to land on your back with the ball clearly off the ground, and you see a friendly team-mate entering the field of vision, by all means give him the ball. The referee won't mind. Several spectators will turn red and whistle through their fingers because they think you should have released the ball after a tackle. But it *wasn't* a tackle, and you know that, and the referee knows that; so who gives a damn about spectators? When did a spectator ever score a try?

Figure 12 *Passing off the ground is perfectly legal* – except when you've been tackled. This player has *not* been tackled, because the ball hasn't touched the ground, and so he's perfectly entitled to lie there and throw it to someone

The working of the tackle law is really very simple and obvious. When play can reasonably go on, the law lets it go on. When the tackled player cannot play the ball, it makes him let go of it so that someone else can play it. And if the ball is on the ground, it's pretty fair to assume that the player came down with such a thump that he couldn't play the ball for a moment.

Mind you, there are also occasions when nobody has laid a finger on you from the knees up and the ball has not touched the ground, but the referee will still consider that you have been tackled, and so will you. Those are the occasions when you are abruptly smashed five yards sideways under the impact of a screaming kamikaze prop forward. At a time when you're not absolutely sure where your head is, you are in no condition to do anything with the ball except drop it. Immediately.

There are two reasons why the law says *immediately*. One is so that other players can grab the ball and keep the game going. The other is so that you aren't turned into a basket case by opponents who are looking for the ball. As usual, what's good for the game is good for the player, too.

Right then, onwards. You are tackled, you let go of the ball. Fine. What next?

The next player to play the ball – whether he picks it up, passes it or kicks it – *must be on his feet*. Rugby is a game where you run with the ball, and you can't run on your knees. That goes for you, for the man who tackled you, and for anyone else who accidentally trips over you both. Find your feet before you look for the ball.

A few pathetically obvious remarks.

Since the law requires the tackled player to let go of the ball, it also requires everyone else to *let* him let go of it. Do not grovel for possession with a tackled man.

Once he has let go of it, he has as much right to the ball as any other upright player. So don't try to stop him from getting up.

Even if you are not the tackler or his victim but you just happen to be lying on the ground taking a close interest in the game, don't interfere with the ball in any way. Don't even reach out and tuck the lace in. *After a tackle, the next player to play the ball must be on his feet.* All right, I know you knew that already; well, now you've no excuse for forgetting it.

There is one exception to all of the above: none of it applies to the in-goal. A tackle, legally speaking, is only a tackle in the field-of-play, which is the bit between the goal-lines. Once you cross the goal-line there is not much point in expecting a bloke to drop the ball just because you've got hold of him, so the law is completely different there. (*See* the chapter on in-goal play.)

Tackling has not always been the humane and enlightened affair it is today. Back in the 1850s, when the game was still a kind of student demonstration at Rugby School, a player who was 'collared' could cry, 'Have it down!' and put the ball on the ground for a scrum. If he didn't, his opponents could shout 'Hack him over!' and start kicking. They hacked only from the knee down, and they weren't allowed to hold *and* hack at the same time; still, they sometimes hacked for up to a quarter of an hour before they got the ball down. Today's law achieves the same result about three hundred times more rapidly and five thousand times less painfully.

The penalty for breaking any part of the tackle law is a penalty kick at the place of infringement.

Three Somebody blundered

All the offences

Four principles sum up the things you must and must not do in Rugby:

1 The only way to gain ground is to run or kick. You must not throw or knock the ball forward.
2 You can grab an opponent, or get in his way, only if he has the ball.
3 Even so, you must not play dangerously.
4 You must do all you can to keep the game as fast-moving and continuous as possible.

If you follow these simple principles, you'll be all right – in theory. Still, it won't do any harm to go through the charge sheet with a powerful lens and a fine-tooth comb, just to reveal the gruesome details.

Throw-forward and knock-on

Penalty: scrum
Throw-forward. You must not throw the ball forward. 'Forward' does not mean 'in front of you'; it means 'towards the enemy line'. (If you have crossed the enemy line and are unselfishly donating the ball to a team-mate, just don't throw it towards the enemy dead-ball line.) Picture an imaginary line running through the ball, parallel to the goal lines, and make your pass go along or behind that line, and you should be all right. If the ball hits the ground and *bounces* forward, your pass is still okay. The laws try to regulate what you do, but nobody on earth can say what a Rugby ball is going to do next.

It has been argued by people who have nothing better to do that when two players are running upfield absolutely level with each other and one gives a pass, the ball must go forward if it is to arrive where and when the other player is due to arrive, even though the first player is still running level with him. Other people disagree, and draw little diagrams with their beer on the top of the bar to prove it by trigonometry.

It doesn't matter terribly much, because when you start cutting it as fine as that, the decision really hinges on how much dust there is in the referee's left eye. That's where all the really important trigonometry takes place. It doesn't much matter whether or not you make a forward pass – what matters is whether the referee *thinks* you did. Moral: make it easy for him to approve.

It is pretty obvious why a forward pass is illegal: anybody on your team who takes one is bound to be off-side, anyway. But note that the law doesn't call it a forward *pass*, but a *throw-forward*. So whether or not anyone catches the thing is beside the point – if it's forward, it's no good.

Knock-on. And if you can't *throw* it forward, then you must not *knock* it forward, either. Stands to reason. To qualify for a knock-on, you don't have to actually *knock* the ball, or punch it, prod it or even give it a good hard slap. A knock-on need be nothing more than a clumsy fumble in the general direction of the enemy camp. The law says that if the ball hits your hand or arm (or *vice versa*) and goes forward, towards your opponents' dead-ball line, then it's a knock-on – whether the ball has travelled half an inch or thirteen feet. With these three exceptions:

The three knock-on exceptions
1 '*Cricket catch*'. If you knock-on, but you manage to catch the ball before it has touched the ground or another player, this is not a knock-on. It makes no difference whether you're fielding a kick or taking a pass or scooping the ball up from

the ground – you can fumble and juggle it till your captain's hair turns white, but provided you don't drop it altogether or let it touch another player, this is not a knock-on.

2 *Fair-catch.* If you knock the ball forward and an opponent makes a fair-catch with it, play goes on. Well, it doesn't, in fact, because the referee whistles for the fair-catch, but he ignores the knock-on.

3 *Kick charged down.* If your opponent now takes his free kick and you – seething with humiliation and remorse –

Figure 13 If you charge down a kick and knock the ball forward, this is not a knock-on (as long as you're not trying to catch it)

succeed in charging down the kick, then it is not a knock-on, even if the ball hits your hand or arm and bounces forward. So now you can feel a bit better.

No deliberate knock-ons
The laws say that a knock-on (or a throw-forward, come to that) must be unintentional. If you interrupt an enemy

pass by sticking your great fist out and deliberately knocking the ball forward, you're asking for a penalty kick. Similarly, if someone slings a wild pass behind you, and you reach back and biff it forward so that you can catch it again, this is obviously not just an accidental fumble; it's a deliberate knock-on, and the laws won't stand for that.

If you must fumble, fumble backwards.

A knock-on does not have to be knocked, but it does have to be *on*. Suppose you take a pass or field a kick when you are facing backwards, towards your own line. You can juggle with the ball, fumble it, drop it – and it's all perfectly legal. The game goes on. Unless the ball bounces *forward* – towards the enemy line – from a hand or arm, then it's not a knock-on.

You will sometimes notice that the wise and seasoned full-back – the sort who always gives his cigarettes to a spectator to hold, knowing that they might get crushed if he were called upon to make a tackle – the experienced full-back, when fielding the enemy's kicks, *turns his body towards his own line* as he cradles the ball. This graceful motion, sometimes compared to the slow-collapse step in the tango, is done to make sure that even if he fumbles the ball and drops it, at least he won't knock it on. Sideways or backwards maybe, but not on.

A couple of laughably obvious points which nobody but a raving perfectionist like yourself would bother to read:

A rebound – off the chest, for example, or the shoulder – is not a knock-on; it's a rebound. If, however, a rebound ricochets off a chest and hits a hand or arm *and then* bounces forward, it *is* a knock-on. What often happens is that a player fails to catch a ball, which hits his chest and bounces forward, leaving him wheezing pitifully, the spectators demanding a knock-on, and the referee, quite rightly, doing nothing.

In case you have just joined us at this point, here is a news

Figure 14 If you unintentionally knock the ball forward but catch it before it touches the ground or another player, this is not a knock-on

Figure 15 One way to avoid risking a knock-on – by turning to the side

summary. A player throws-forward or knocks-on when he throws or knocks (or even fumbles) the ball in the direction of his opponents' dead-ball line – unless (in the case of a knock-on) he catches it again before it touches the ground or another player. And the penalty for this lapse is a scrum at the place of shame, his opponents having the benefit of putting the ball in.

And now, back to our regular programme.

Charging and Obstruction,
or – even worse – Foul Play and Misconduct

The difference between *Charging and Obstruction*, on the one hand, and *Foul Play and Misconduct*, on the other, is this.

Charging and Obstruction is trying to play the right game the wrong way and – if caught – you get penalized with a penalty kick.

Foul Play and Misconduct is not playing the game at all, and if you're lucky you only get warned and penalized with a penalty kick. Do it again and, if you're lucky, you get penalized with a penalty kick, exiled to the changing room, and eventually carpeted. (If you're unlucky you get a large knuckle sandwich.)

This distinction between *C and O, and FP and M*, tells us a lot about the laws and what they're out to do.

The laws are against unfair play of any kind, and wherever it rears its ugly head the lawbook delivers a crisp penalty kick. But if the player was taking a positive part in the game when he committed his black act, the laws consider a penalty kick enough. 'The lad did wrong,' they reason patiently, 'but at least he wanted to get on with the game. Now perhaps he'll know better.'

Whereas the bloke who does something utterly foolish, negative, dangerous or pernicious is really sabotaging the game; he is not so much playing bad Rugby as playing anti-Rugby, so he's a menace to all concerned, and the laws not only penalize his team with a penalty kick but also warn him or send him off. 'That joker is going to spoil it for everyone,' they brood, worriedly. 'If he wants to indulge his sordid whims he'd better take up bingo, or television wrestling. Next time he tries to throttle the scrum-half, have him quietly removed.'

First, then, *Charging and Obstruction*. Exactly what . . . ?
1 *Running for the ball*. When you are running for the ball, and an opponent is also running for the ball, you must not

charge him or push him *except shoulder to shoulder*. Now, you very rarely see this shoulder-to-shoulder stuff done, and when you do somebody in the crowd usually takes exception to it; nevertheless it's perfectly legal as long as you keep running for the ball. It can be very effective, too, especially if the other bloke trips over his own feet.

Figure 16 If you and an opponent are both running for the ball, it's perfectly legal to charge him – but it must be shoulder-to-shoulder, and you must keep running

2 *Flank-forwards swinging out from a scrum.* When your side has hooked the ball in a scrum and it is coming out of the back row, the flank-forwards – what the law calls 'outside players' – must not swing further outwards to stop the opposing scrum-half from coming round and zeroing in on your scrum-half (if he's got the ball) or the ball itself (if he hasn't).

There's nothing, except the length of his arms, to stop a flank-forward from packing on to the scrum at a wide angle if he wants to. The law simply says that, once the ball has been heeled, he must not move out to an even wider angle.

Nor may he stand up from the scrum and have a good stretch at this crucial moment. It's remarkable how some

Figure 17 *Illegal!* A flank-forward (No. 6 here) must not try to prevent the opposing scrum-half from getting past by swinging out from the scrum. The flank-forward can pack at any angle, but he must not then widen the angle

quite scrawny flank-forwards seem to fill out and develop extra arms and legs when the opposing scrum-half is trying to get past them. They blink at the light and don't quite know what to do with themselves, so they stay where they are, occupying about seventeen square yards of turf. This is obstruction, and wrong.

3 *Off-side player obstructing opponent.* If you are in front of a player on your own side who has the ball (which makes you off-side, right?), you must not stand or move in such a way that you obstruct an opponent who's trying to get at him. This is pretty obvious: if you're off-side, you have no business interfering with the course of the game. Notice that it's up to you to *avoid* interfering with play. It is possible to obstruct an opponent simply by *being* in his way as well as by *getting* in his way. If you're off-side and in his way at all, it's your job to get out of it – not his job to go around you.

4 *Running into your own scrum or line-out.* If you have the ball after a scrum or line-out, you must not try and crash through your own forwards in front of you. It's obvious: they must be off-side, and you are bringing them into the game. Slightly less obviously, you are using them as a shield to keep the horny hands of the enemy off you; and since in Rugby every man should be free to grab the man with the ball, provided he can catch him, what you are doing is wrong.

Nevertheless, it's amazing how many players cannot resist taking the shortest route to the enemy line by ploughing straight through their own forwards – a short cut which is, to say the least, short-sighted.

Penalty

The penalty for charging or obstruction is a penalty kick at the place of infringement.

Second, *Foul Play and Misconduct.* Precisely how . . . ?
1 *Don't touch him unless he's got the ball.* This gets right to

the heart of the matter. If Rugby is to be a wide-open, man-to-man contest for a bit of streamlined leather, people have got to be free to try to intercept the ball (or the ball-carrier) just as fast as their puny limbs and wheezing lungs can carry them. What you cannot have is other players reaching and pawing at them, lurching into them and seizing handfuls of hair, clothing or fatty tissue, or simply sneaking up behind and unloading a large shove in the small of the back. I mean, it's hard enough to run right across a Rugby field after a heavy meal and wearing someone else's boots, without being got at by some grasping saboteur who isn't even looking for the ball.

Similarly it is wrong to obstruct an opponent who hasn't got the ball and wants it, simply by being or getting in his way. Sometimes, of course, it's difficult to get *out* of his way until you know which way he's going; but not always. If you are standing right between him and your team-mate who has just caught the ball and fallen flat on his face with it, don't put your hands on your hips and wait to be asked to move. Just move.

Keen students of the printed word will be asking themselves, at this point, if they haven't been here before. Doesn't it all seem terribly familiar? A sense of what the French call *déjà vu*? (It's all right, they play Rugby too.) Well, yes and no. Our recent skirmish with the law of Charging and Obstruction included a warning against off-side players obstructing opponents by getting or being between them and the ball. That's what you're thinking of. Why then, you ask, go over the whole grisly mess again? Two reasons.

First, there is a difference. The Charging and Obstruction offence talks about *off-side* players who *obstruct* an opponent. The Foul Play and Misconduct offence covers *any* player, off-side or on, who obstructs *or lays hands on* an opponent. Now this is much worse. It is at least understandable that an off-side player – by definition usually in front of a team-mate with the ball – might get in an opponent's way. It's wrong and it can't be allowed to pass, but it's understandable. But a player who hasn't even the excuse of being off-side, and who not only obstructs an opponent but actually tries to distract him from the game by using force – now there is a bloke who is asking for trouble. He's in line for a penalty kick plus a warning or even a sending-off. There is just no room in the game for private revenge. If you can't get the man with the ball, then don't get anybody.

That's the second reason for re-hashing this subject. It is important because it is absolutely basic, and therefore worth repeating a few times. The simple charm of Rugby is that anyone can lay claim to the ball, and everyone else enjoys the same freedom to go after him and get it back. Don't try and stop them.

And don't imagine you can get around the law by grabbing a player's jersey instead of the player. Clothing counts, too.

In fact it hurts to have to tell you that there is one occasion, when you can, lawfully, hold an opponent who hasn't got the ball, and that is in a scrum. You can also drag away a player who is lying close to the ball – but *not* in a scrum or ruck.

Don't get too excited about it, though. As privileges go, this is worth about as much as sitting next to the driver on the bus.

Besides, your opponent can do it to you, too.

2 *And don't obstruct him after he's kicked the ball, either.* If you think you've also been *there* before, well, so you have. This is more of the same old stuff about not charging, tackling, holding, prodding, barging or in any way molesting a player who hasn't got the ball – in this case, an opponent who hasn't got it because he has just kicked it.

What is so special about this offence is the penalty: *either* a penalty kick at the place where you did it *or* a penalty kick at the spot where the ball comes down. Intriguing, no?

Figure 18 The penalty for obstructing a player after he's kicked the ball gives the kicker's team a choice – a penalty kick *either* where the obstruction took place *or* where the ball landed. Not much doubt which one they chose here

The thinking behind this piece of law is as follows. Suppose you are a threequarter doing your fleetfoot stuff down the wing, ball neatly tucked under the outside arm. Out of the corner of your eye you see an opponent, hurtling in for a tackle. Meanwhile, hobbling at top speed down the middle, as you know from past experience, is your entire pack of forwards, baying for blood. It is but the work of a moment to extract the ball from the armpit and cross-kick it smartly into their immediate future – say; about fifteen yards in front of them.

Eager to the point of rashness, of course, they are all – every sweating buffoon of them – yards off-side at the moment you kick the ball. So it's up to you to carry on flashing down the wing until you've caught up with them and put them on-side.

Right now is when your opponent, foiled of his tackle, runs directly in your path. Obstruction, of course; but look at the effect! Not only has he stopped you from taking part in the game; he has also effectively stopped you from putting your forwards on-side. So he has quietly killed your brilliant cross-kick, and with it perhaps a chance of a try. By God, skinning with a blunt putty-knife is too good for the swine.

What the law lays down, to discourage this kind of obstruction, is that the innocent party can choose to take its penalty kick in one of two places, as already described. If the player who obstructed the kicker did so to nullify a cross-kick, then the law makes sure he fails by giving his opponents the chance of a penalty kick in the middle, where the ball landed. On the other hand, it may be that the cross-kick was a wild one and came down in a poor place from which to take a penalty, so they have the option of taking it from the spot where the player was obstructed.

You can see this would work out just as well if the kicker put in a kick-ahead instead of a cross-kick, before he was obstructed. And there's always the penalty-try law, which might apply if the obstruction were a desperate, last-ditch affair.

In case anybody is wondering what happens if the cross-kick or kick-ahead comes down in touch, or near touch, or in the in-goal, or in touch-in-goal, or on or over the dead-ball line, the answer is that the mark for the penalty kick is given at a fair place on the field-of-play, as decided by the referee in accordance with a formula which is far too complicated for you to strain your brains on. Just take his word for it.

3 *No hacking, kicking or tripping.* The law today is simple: do not kick, or trip, an opponent at any time. It was not always so.

As late as 1866, all that the laws of the game as played at

Rugby School said about hacking was that you could not do it on or above the knee or with the heel, and you couldn't hold *and* hack, unless, of course, the victim stupidly refused to release the ball, in which case you could settle down and batter him to a pulp.

In 1874 the Rugby Football Union declared that hacking and tripping were absolutely prohibited under all circumstances, a sure sign that a lot of it was still going on.

Today, of course, hacking is definitely out . . . Well, let's not get carried away; you don't see many manufacturers of shin-pads selling matches in the street; so let's say that any hacking is accidental rather than intentional.

Tripping, by the way, is done with the foot. If you trip over somebody's hand or arm, that's your fault, not his.

4 *No striking opponents*. And it's no good saying you hit him because he wouldn't let go of the ball: you are not allowed to thump *any* opponent, with or without the ball, at *any* time.

Players on your own side are different; the laws have nothing against clouting them . . . unless, of course, you are both off-side and your colleague falls senseless in the path of an opponent with the ball, in which case unintentional obstruction might perhaps . . . No. On the whole, it's safer not to belt anyone.

5 *No dangerous tackling*. The two particularly grisly tackles which all referees hate, despise and won't stand for are:

a the early tackle, when the victim is looking the other way because that's where the ball is coming from;
b the late tackle, when the victim has relaxed and is vulnerable and looking the other way, because that's where the ball has gone.

These are stupid and dangerous tackles. They are dangerous because it is tragically easy to damage a player by tackling him when he hasn't a chance to tense his body for the shock.

(In this respect, a late tackle can be even worse than an early one, because the player has *relaxed* after giving his pass.) And they are stupid because the tackler invariably knows that the man hasn't got the ball, and even if he can't avoid making some kind of a tackle he need not go in full blast.

Figure 19 *Illegal and dangerous!* An early tackle – like this – is as illegal and dangerous as a late tackle, and it's the responsibility of the player to avoid making either of them

This is one of the responsibilities of playing Rugby. Only the player can control the strength and timing of his impact. Nobody expects a tackle to be pleasant or even painless, and one of the hazards of jinking your way through for a brilliant solo try is getting rudely dumped on your ass in the middle of it. But let us remember why we are playing this game; what the object is. The aim in Rugby is to win the ball and score with it. You get no thanks and no points for putting a player out of action. It's getting the ball that counts.

Once you find yourself making a tackle *in order to injure the player*, instead of *in order to get the ball from him*, then you are heading for a disaster the memory of which you may have to live with for the rest of your life. And what good has it done? Even if you win the game, can you honestly say that you have beaten a team when you had more players than they did?

Last word on this subject: the laws have laid down that it is dangerous for a player to tap or pull the feet of an opponent as he is jumping in a line-out. This is considered illegal. And quite right too. It *is* dangerous.

6 *Don't collapse the scrum.* Telling a forward not to collapse the scrum is like telling a human pyramid not to scratch itself: horribly obvious. And yet it needs to be said, because you do occasionally see forwards doing it, usually when their opponents have won the ball and are trudging relentlessly towards a pushover try.

Well, it's no good; you must not intentionally collapse a scrum. (If you merely come to pieces under the strain, that's different.) It's dangerous, and it negates the whole purpose of having a scrum, which is to have a scrum until the scrum is over. In this respect it's rather like travelling on the Underground, going to cocktail parties, or making love: they're all scrums, and you simply have to see them through to the end.

7 *Don't start anything while the ball is out of play.* This is one of those splendidly vague laws which every civilized nation keeps tucked away in its hip pocket to deal with lunatics and hot-heads. It simply says that, while the ball is out of play, you must not obstruct, or molest, or interfere with, or spit at, or denounce, or make up disgusting limericks about, any opponent. Nor must you commit any sort of misconduct. (Try and get round *that*.)

The penalty kick is given, not where the offence took place, but where the ball would next have been brought into play. If, for instance, your opponents kicked the ball over your goal line and you touched it down, and an opponent came up and molested you right in the solar plexus, you would take the penalty kick from your 25-yard line, since you would otherwise have had a drop-out. If the ball goes into touch and there's some hanky-panky before it's thrown in, the penalty kick is given fifteen yards in from touch.

Finally – and just to lumber your echoing skull with a scrap of data which you will probably never use – if the referee gives a penalty kick, or allows a free kick, and an opponent blows a fuse before the kick is taken, the referee awards a second penalty kick, ten yards in front of the first kick, and this second kick replaces the first one.

In this and all other cases of Foul Play and Misconduct – whether it's tackling or obstructing a man without the ball, hacking, tripping, striking, dangerous play or scrum-collapsing – the penalty kick is only half the penalty. The referee can send the player off, there and then. If not, he *must* warn him; and if the player does it again, he *must* send him off. That means he stays off for the rest of the game and – depending on the Disciplinary Committee's feelings – probably for several other games, too.

Wasting time (penalty: penalty kick)

There are several ways to waste time in Rugby, and they're all stupid. They're stupid for two reasons:

a If you don't want to play you shouldn't be out there in the first place; and

b If the referee sees you he'll penalize you.

Nevertheless, it's surprising how many players do it. Maybe they are feeling rather jaded. Maybe they've scored five tries already that afternoon and they're getting bored. Or maybe they just don't think about it. Take, for instance . . .

1 *Wasting time by not getting on with it.* Many players waste a great deal of time simply by not doing all they could to get on with the game. There is a slow way to put the ball into a scrum, and a fast way. The slow way is for the forwards to pack down and the scrum-half to start looking for the ball. When he locates it – cleverly camouflaged on that patch of mud, ten yards away – he *walks* over to it, picks it up, drops it, retrieves it, reads the name on it in case it's the wrong ball, tucks the lace in, and *walks* slowly back to the scrum.

Correct me if my arithmetic is wrong; but that leaves sixteen forwards heaving and sweating, and thirteen backs standing around scratching themselves, while one scrum-half carries on the game at a steady limp. I don't care if he is getting his breath back, it's still a pathetic waste of twenty-nine players' time. What's more, it is, strictly speaking, illegal.

The laws are liberally spattered with the key phrase, 'without delay'. The ball must be put into the scrum without delay. In fact, the laws say that it shall be put in without delay *as soon as the two front rows have closed together*. So any scrum-half who waits until a flank-forward has finished blowing his nose and leaned on the nearest rump before he puts the ball in, is wasting time. Any wing-threequarter who waits until his pack leader has finished an inspiring harangue, before throwing the ball into a line-out, is wasting time. Any team which is awarded a penalty kick and then democratically debates what to do with it, is wasting time. Nobody ever scored a try while the ball was out of play.

I am not suggesting that everything should be done at the gallop. All I'm saying is that, if players were as alert when the ball is dead as they are when it is alive, then we would see shorter stoppages and more game. (Amazingly, even at International level, the ball is actually in play for only about one-third of the game.) As it is, they often seem to regard the sound of the whistle as a signal to stop thinking.

The referee has a duty, under the laws, to see that the game goes forward 'without delay', and if he thinks you're acting unnecessarily sluggishly, he is right to award a penalty kick just to goose you along a bit. And the fact that you didn't *know* you were acting all constipated is neither here nor there: one disadvantage of sluggishness is that very often you are too sluggish to realize just how sluggish you are.

After all that, it will come as no great surprise to you to learn that deliberately wasting time stands no chance at all of getting past the referee. The more obvious way of doing it is by kicking the ball in the wrong direction, for example when your opponents have just been given a penalty kick. The less obvious methods we shall now explain.

2 *Wasting time by breaking a small law.* Suppose you are given the ball inside your own 25 at a moment when three large opponents are bearing down on you from the left, and two huge opponents are thundering towards you from the front.

As you have just sprained your ankle, it seems unlikely that you will evade them all. Inevitably, you will be tackled, they'll get the ball, and then nothing stands between them and your line but twenty feet of thin autumn mist.

Suddenly you see a team-mate to your right. He's six feet in front of you, but unmarked. If you give him a forward pass the referee is bound to notice, and a scrum at least gives your side a chance to re-group. So you deliberately throw the ball forward.

The referee whistles and gives your opponents a penalty kick. Rugby is based on the assumption that the players will try to uphold the laws, even when they are feeling desperate. If you intentionally break a law for which the usual penalty is only a scrum, you are distorting the game, and you will be made to suffer for it.

3 *Wasting time by throwing into touch*. If you want to put the ball in touch you must either dispatch it by boot or accompany it in person. Deliberately throwing it into touch from the field-of-play is the easy way out. This also applies to throwing it from the field-of-play into touch-in-goal or over the dead-ball line. The penalty is a penalty kick.

4 *Wasting time by lying on the ball*. This exercise is not to be confused with *falling* on the ball. Falling on the ball usually stops a forward rush, and is all right. Lying on the ball inevitably stops the entire game, and is all wrong.

Once you have fallen on the ball it doesn't much matter what you do as long as you get on and do it. You can get up and run with the ball, or stay down and kick it, or pass

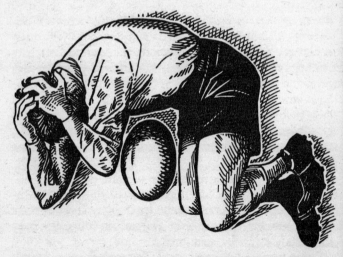

Figure 20 *Illegal!* It's not enough to avoid lying on the ball – you must also do all you can to get up or roll away from it. This player isn't even touching the ball, but he's certainly preventing others from getting at it just as much as if he were lying on it

it, or let go and get out of the way – anything as long as you do it *at once*. And if you're not going to play the ball you must, if you can, get up or roll away from it.

What you must *not* do is drape yourself over the ball and lie there until help comes. Even if you are the last defender and the enemy is two feet from the line, you must not lie on the ball. It ruins the game and – unless the referee blows up smartly – it may do considerable damage to you, too.

Persistent offending

The laws of Rugby are a description of the game. Change the description, and you change the game.

Players who persistently break a law are, in effect, trying to change the game. They may be doing it for their own advantage, e.g. by barging in the line-out. Or they may be doing it simply because they don't know any better. (There are hookers like that.) The effect is the same: it distorts the game, and by distorting it, spoils it for everyone.

A player who is constantly penalized for off-side does more damage than the penalty kicks can pay for, because he is obstructing his opponents when they are trying to launch attacks. The man is a menace. Similarly, the prop forward who won't let the ball into the scrum is damaging the chances of *both* teams to get on with the game. And ignorance is no excuse: the damage is the same whether he knows what he's doing, or not.

That is why the referee is given powers to deal with this sort of thing. Not surprisingly, he is required to apply a stricter standard in senior matches: when a player breaks the same law for the third time, the referee must warn him about it, and if that doesn't work he can even send him off. In more junior Rugby, where the percentage of goons is higher, the referee usually warns the player first and then, if he doesn't improve, warns his captain that the player will have to go off unless he can be rendered harmless. The captain, if he has any brains, gives the offender an immediate posting to the wing, followed by an early lesson on the game.

Four Scrums, rucks and mauls

Including off-side

1 Scrums

I could write a whole book about scrums, and most of it would be junk.

It's one part of the game that has been turned into a special subject all on its own. Some people become experts in the scrum the way others spend their lives learning all there is to know about wallpaper, or the sex-life of the bloater. And it's about as big a waste of time as eating gravy with your fork.

Scrums are very simple. There is no secret about them. You can understand all, provided you use a little common sense and remember the ancient Chinese saying:

Only reason for scrum is re-starting game quickly and fairly

Now, then. If that is its purpose, what is its shape? We all know what a scrum looks like – eight compressed men growing shorter and wider in an effort to telescope eight other compressed men – but what must you have, and what can you do without? It is (as you're probably starting to discover) All Quite Simple.

What is a scrum?

A scrum must have at least six men in it: two opposing front rows of three players each. As soon as these three-man front rows have ducked their heads and come together, that's it – you have a scrum. And the law says that from this moment the scrum-half *shall* put the ball in *without delay*.

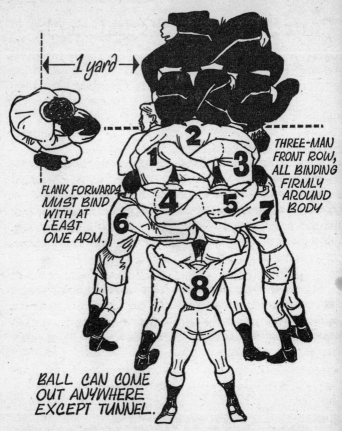

← 1 yard →

THREE-MAN FRONT ROW, ALL BINDING FIRMLY AROUND BODY

FLANK FORWARDS MUST BIND WITH AT LEAST ONE ARM.

BALL CAN COME OUT ANYWHERE EXCEPT TUNNEL.

Figure 21 Bird's-eye view of a scrum. Note that the scrum-half stands one yard from it. He puts the ball in fairly, along a midway line where the shoulders of the opposing front rows meet. Each flank-forward (6 and 7) binds around the body of the second row (4 or 5). It's not enough for a flank-forward to rest his hand in the middle of this player's back, or grab a handful of jersey near his shoulder-blades. The flank-forward must bind *around the body* – and stay bound as long as he is part of the scrum

All it takes, then, to make a scrum is the two front rows. If the scrum-half hangs around, biting his lip and waiting for the other forwards to pack down, he is wasting time. He should be penalized for it.

Players often get upset about this, and usually for one of two reasons. They argue either that the scrum-half has to trundle off and get the ball, which takes time, or that the other forwards have to trundle over and add themselves behind their front row, which also takes time.

Both observations are true as far as they go. What they overlook is the fact that scrum-halves and lock forwards can hustle pretty damn fast when they really want to. If they would only put a bit of ginger into their trundling then half a second after the front rows went down the other five forwards would be locked on to it. And half a second later the scrum-half would have the ball in.

It all depends on your attitude. If you regard a scrum as a kind of tea-break – a chance to lean on someone and get your breath back – then obviously there is no hurry. If you regard it as a piece of well-greased machinery for getting the ball into play, then you want to see it working pretty damn fast.

Without cursing and blinding in my uncontrollable fashion, the laws leave no doubt that they are against tea-breaks.

The front row

The front rows are the heart of a scrum. This is where it all happens. The rest is just horsepower.

Each front row must have three players in it – no more and no less. These three must link together firmly, so that they don't fall apart, and must combine properly with their opponents, so that nobody dislocates anything.

This means that the front rows must not form up some distance apart and charge each other. (An Irish forward actually broke his neck doing this in 1924.) And it means that the players must interlock naturally, with opposing heads next to each other. Two front-row players of the same team with their idiot heads locked together just break everything apart.

The law about binding does two jobs. It keeps the front

Figure 22 The heads of the two front rows must interlock so that adjacent heads belong to opposing teams

row intact, and it stops the hooker from swinging like a trapeze artist.

Every player in the front row must bind, and keep on binding, around his mate's body. The props latch on to their hooker, the hooker clamps both arms around his props – with both arms either under *or* over his props' arms, but not a bit of both. They must all bind around the body – *not* across the shoulders – so that they grip at or below armpit-level. If they do this properly, the scrum won't disintegrate and the hooker cannot swing into the middle of his opponents' second row.

The tunnel

The only reason for having the two front rows is to form a tunnel for putting the ball into, quickly and fairly. Therefore, like all good tunnels, this one must be open and dependable.

All front-row players must have their feet on the ground. Their feet must not be crossed, and they must be in a position to shove. That is what the law says. It doesn't say

Figure 23 Scrum-half's view of the tunnel, showing (more or less) how the front-row players must have their feet back and in a position to shove, thus keeping the tunnel open for the entry of the ball down the middle

they have to shove, but it does say they have to be *in a position* to shove, and to shove forward.

A quick experiment against the nearest wall will prove that the only way to shove forward is to place the feet towards the rear. How far to the rear is a matter of taste, but an angle of forty-five degrees is one that appeals to many referees with long experience in the shoving business.

Other referees feel that forty-three degrees is quite adequate, or that on a wet day forty-nine degrees is the absolute minimum. It's all a bit academic, because the law also says that front-row players must keep their feet back far enough to allow a clear tunnel, come rain or shine. So that clinches it.

Keep your size elevens pulled back so that the referee can see plenty of daylight on the other side, and you'll be all right.

If all this makes the front row of a scrum sound as balanced and sober as a Baptist missionary reunion, that is unfortunate, because it doesn't work out that way. Veins bulge, joints crack, discs slip, strange animal noises are heard, and – to paraphrase Dylan Thomas – steam comes gushing out of their nostrils. Considerable heaving and grinding take place.

Nevertheless, despite all the sado-masochism, the front rows have a duty to keep the tunnel standing and open. The hooker, for instance, must not hang entirely from his props: some of his weight must always be on his own feet. And a prop must not use his free arm to push or pull the opposing prop, but only to hold himself (and the scrum) steady; and the free arm of the loose-head prop on the team putting in the ball must be *inside* the free arm of the tight-head prop opposing him. That ruling avoids a lot of ill-tempered wrestling.

Similarly, a front-row player must not at any time – either before or after the ball is in – take both feet off the ground at once, or deliberately do anything else that might make the scrum collapse, such as twisting his body or forcing it downwards. And once the ball is in the tunnel, he must not kick it back out again.

This is all pretty obvious. A scrum is to heel the ball. You can't have people deliberately preventing either the scrum or the heel from taking place.

The second and back rows

Or, if you like, the second, third, fourth and back rows. There is no upper limit to the number of players you can have in a scrum. All fifteen can get down and shove, if they want to. The only requirement is that they must bind. You are not in a scrum unless you have at least one hand and arm *around the body* of a team-mate. You don't have to shove, but you must keep a firm grip on his rib-cage. Resting your hand lightly on the small of his back is not binding, either legally or physically.

If you are a flank-forward, packing in a 3–4–1 formation, you must bind around the second row, not the prop. This goes back to the principle of a three-man front row. A flank-forward who attaches himself to a prop-forward is creating a *four*-man front row. That way, as they used to say in Victorian novels, madness lies. Another thing: as long as the ball is in the tunnel, only the front-row players may play it. No poaching by the second row.

Not surprisingly, second- and back-row forwards must not do any of the things which front-row forwards are not allowed to do. They must not collapse the scrum, or deliberately fall down, and if the ball comes out of the scrum they must not put it back in. Nobody at all is allowed to handle the ball in a scrum, and that covers picking it up with your legs. (Why would anyone want to? Vanity? Boredom? Mental breakdown?)

Scrums: *where?*

You can have a scrum anywhere in the field-of-play, and nowhere else. So touchlines and goal-lines are death to scrums.

The scrum should go down as near as possible to where the stoppage happened. If this is near touch, the referee will make sure that *all* the scrum is in the field-of-play. If the mark is near the goal-line, he will make sure that at least the defending front row is in the field-of-play. You know that two front rows are all you need to form a scrum. The second and back rows can sprawl well inside the in-goal as long as the front row is over the line.

The scrum must stay where it went down until the ball goes in, and it must be fairly square, too – not in shape but in position. All this is obvious. The game has to be re-started more or less where it stopped, and any pack which tries to shove its opponents into the car park before the ball is put in is simply wasting its time, because the referee will bring them back to the mark. Similarly, he will make sure that the scrum is fairly square – i.e. that the tunnel is more or less parallel with the goal-lines – before he lets the scrum-half put the ball in.

And now – for I see that the scrum-half has, at last, retrieved the ball from the sewage farm behind the pavilion – we might let him have a little go at stuffing it up the tunnel.

Putting the ball in
This, it goes without saying, he should do honestly and fairly, so that both hookers get a good chance to hook the

Figure 24 Scrum-half about to put the ball into a scrum. Note that both hands hold the ball midway between the legs and midway between knee and ankle. From this position he must put the ball in straight, without feinting or 'dummying' his put-in

ball, and before we go any further I just want to say that if there is any more of that coarse, cynical laughter I shall go back to writing TV commercials. It's not my fault that all scrum-halves are cheats, rogues and con men. It must be something to do with their genes.

Mind you, the law as it is written doesn't leave the scrum-half much room for manoeuvre, although this hasn't noticeably stopped him trying. What it says is this:

The scrum-half must stand one yard from the scrum. (He may choose which side of the scrum to stand, but if he has any brains he will put the ball in on his loose-head prop's side – normally the left. Having chosen, he must stick to it.) He must stand midway between the two front rows. He must hold the ball in both hands midway between his knee and his ankle. Then, *without feinting or moving the ball back*, he must put the ball quickly straight down the middle of the tunnel – that is, along a line where the opposing front rows' shoulders meet – so that it touches the ground just past the first prop-forward. So it has got to travel at least the width of the prop's shoulders into the scrum.

And until it touches the ground, no front-row forward may raise a foot.

You would think that that spelt it all out clearly enough, wouldn't you? You would think everything was buttoned up and nailed down and fenced securely in, beyond a doubt or a peradventure. And yet getting the ball into the scrum causes more problems than any other single aspect of the game. Players complain that no two referees apply the same interpretation. Referees complain that players don't follow the law. And spectators just complain, not that anyone cares about them.

If it's any consolation, life was always thus. Down through the years men have aged and withered under the strain of finding a better way to put the ball into the scrum. In 1920 New Zealand suggested that the referee should do the job. In 1929 the International Board thought scrum-halves were standing too far away and throwing too hard. In 1931 the law was changed to make the scrum-half 'gently propel' the ball in. That didn't work very well, and next year the IB warned against 'throwing the ball into the scrummage with unnecessary force'. In 1934 the Rugby Football Union was explaining that 'gently propel' now meant that 'the ball is not put in at excessive speed'. In 1937 the scrum-half was told to put the ball in 'fairly, at moderate speed'. That didn't work, either, and in 1939 an RFU committee suggested scrapping everything and just telling the scrum-half to stand a yard away and pitch the thing in, since that was what he was doing anyway. Ulster wanted the speed to be 'slow' instead of 'moderate'. Wales, however, liked 'moderate'. Scotland ignored the speed question and asked for several other changes. Leinster, Munster and Connaught each had their own ideas, and so did Hitler.

Hitler's proposals held attention until 1946, when the entire scrum law was considerably tidied up. This worked quite well, and in 1947 a South African suggestion that the ball be *rolled* into the scrum got nowhere, thank God.

The law today says that the ball should be put in quickly, and if you want to know what that means, it means 'at a quick speed as distinct from a slow speed'; so you can see that things haven't changed all that much.

The best advice for any scrum-half is simply to try and look at things from the referee's point of view occasionally. What does the referee want? He wants the scrum-half to get on with it and put the ball in as soon as the scrum is ready. He wants him to put it in hard enough to get past the loose-head prop, but not so hard that it rockets out the other side.

He would *like* him to put it in fairly – straight down the middle line of the tunnel – but he will usually settle for having it put in not too unfairly. He will let you steal an inch or so because, after all, the scrum itself is moving; but if you try and shoot the ball under your hooker's feet *and* the referee's eye, he is likely to feel insulted. It all boils down to this: don't be greedy.

Hooking the ball; foot-up

The ball must go into the scrum fairly (or not too unfairly), and it must come out in a similar way.

By common consent the hooker is responsible for this, since nobody can move until the ball has touched the ground beyond the loose-head prop, and the hooker is the next man in line. But the law which governs the hooker's actions also applies to the rest of the front-row players.

The hooker must not strike until the ball has touched the ground. After that he can go for the ball with either foot, provided he doesn't take both feet off the ground at once.

You will recall that the scrum-half is under orders to put the ball in quickly. People have calculated that if he does, and if it goes where it should, and if the hooker does not strike until it touches the ground, then the whole thing is impossible because the ball will have flashed across his bows before he can get a foot to it, such being the laws of nature. Other people have proved the same thing with motion pictures of the ball beating the hooker comfortably and barely getting trapped by the far-side props as it makes its bid for freedom.

What they are getting at is that any hooker who actually hooks the ball first time must have struck too soon, and thus be guilty of foot-up. It may be so. Nevertheless, every week-end thousands of hookers do manage to satisfy the referee *and* hook the ball, so there must be a way. What that way is, exactly, is something to be forged in the heat of battle; but a handy slice of advice for hookers is the same as the maxim for scrum-halves: don't be greedy.

Purists may consider that cynical, but then no purist was ever a hooker. Or *vice versa*.

Hookers tend to be the forgotten men of Rugby, rather like miners, doing cramped and exhausting work where no one can see; so they might appreciate this small historical note, just to show that things could be worse. At least as late as 1889 the object of a scrum was not to hook the

Figure 25 *Illegal!* This is a scrum-half's view of a bad case of foot-up. Instead of letting the ball get right inside the tunnel first, the hooker has struck almost as soon as the ball leaves his scrum-half's hands

ball backwards but to hack it forwards, until you had kicked it right through your opponents. This might take some time – five minutes, ten? – because what with all the hacking going on, somebody was bound to miss the ball, and that might lead to deplorable retaliation, which in turn provoked more of the same, so that even when the ball did come out, views continued to be exchanged quite frankly and fearlessly in the depths of the meeting. Today's scrums have their share of crunch, but at least it's a short, sharp crunch.

Heeling the ball

One reason why it's short and sharp is that it is now very easy to heel the ball from the scrum. It can come out anywhere except by the tunnel. You can heel the ball out between the prop's legs, or between the prop and the flank-forward, or through the flank-forward, or the second row – anywhere at all, as long as it's behind the tunnel. The scrum-half can put the ball in and have it heeled out to him half a second later, only a couple of feet away.

If the ball comes back out of the tunnel, the same scrum-half puts it in again, and on the same side. This applies if it goes right through the tunnel. If the prop on the far side sticks out a foot so that the ball goes behind it, this is *not* heeling, and the ball gets put in again.

If the ball is heeled back by the second row, the number eight forward can detach himself from the scrum and pick it up, even though it is in front of him. By breaking from the scrum, he has in fact placed the ball outside it. Similarly, if a flank-forward sees the ball come out of the scrum in front of him he can unbind and snap it up. By that time the scrum is over, anyway.

Picking the ball out

Normally, of course, it's the scrum-half who does the snapping-up, and he does it only when the ball has come right out of the scrum. Handling the ball in the scrum, you will remember, is illegal, and that goes for the scrum-half as much as the forwards. If his forwards heel the ball with all the free-flowing ease of cold treacle, that's just too bad: he'll have to wait for it. Even if it's lying right between his number eight's feet, within easy reach, the scrum-half must let it come to him, and not go in after it.

There is an easy test to decide whether or not a scrum-half is picking the ball out of a scrum. You say to yourself: if the ball were left where it is, and if an opponent were to come thundering round the scrum, would he be off-side? If the answer is yes, then the ball is still in the scrum.

Not every scrum-half thinks this way. A good few feel that the ball is in the scrum until such time as they pick it

Figure 26 Ball in, ball out. In (a) the ball is still in the scrum, so the scrum-half cannot handle it. In (b) the No. 8 forward has moved his right foot up so that the ball is now out, and the scrum-half can pick it up

out. It's an attractive theory, if you're a scrum-half, but not if you're an opponent – or a referee.

Scrum off-side

There are two separate off-side laws for scrums. One applies only to the scrum-halves. The other applies to everyone else.

For scrum-halves, the off-side line runs through the ball itself. As long as the ball is in the scrum, each scrum-half must stay on his own side of it.

This can make life a bit difficult for the scrum-half whose side *has not* heeled the ball. There he is, edging his way around the perimeter of the pack, trying to stay on-side and yet also trying to get close enough to pounce when his opposite number grabs the ball. If he is too eager he will overstep the ball while it is still in the scrum; if he is too cautious it will pop out while he's out of range. He has to walk the fine line between giving away a penalty kick and giving away possession.

This assumes that the ball is heeled quickly, something

OFF-SIDE LINE FOR SCRUM-HALVES

OFF-SIDE LINE FOR BACKS.

Figure 27 Scrum off-side lines. While the ball is in the scrum, each scrum-half must stay on his own side of the ball. All other players not in the scrum (i.e. the backs) must stay behind the tail-end of the scrum until the ball comes out

which last happened in November 1937. When the ball comes back slowly, the scrum-half on the non-heeling side has more time in which to follow it through. However, even if he can see it, he must not try to kick it out of the scrum. Both scrum-halves are forbidden to kick the ball while it's still in the scrum. What's more, the scrum-half who *didn't* put the ball in is not allowed to circle around to the *opposite* side of the scrum and patrol that area. On that side, he can go no further than the rest of his backs – which means staying behind the tail-end of the scrum, until the ball is out.

Not so the scrum-half who put the ball into the scrum, though. He is free to stroll around to the opposite side whenever he likes (provided, of course, he stays behind the ball in the scrum). And if his forwards are skilled enough to channel the ball out through the south-east corner of the scrum, there's precious little the opposing scrum-half can do to prevent him from snapping it up and putting it to work, what with that back row shielding him like a set of flying buttresses. It all means that any pack of forwards which is good enough to hook the ball and heel it intelligently can pretty well guarantee their scrum-half perfect possession.

It has been argued in some quarters that, in the case of a very quick heel, the scrum-half might well be off-side simply because he hasn't had a chance to get behind the ball. He puts the ball in and turns to his right and snaps it up as it's heeled out – *between him and his goal-line*. On paper, it's an argument that is hard to fault; but it's only fair to add that you don't meet many referees who apply it on the field.

For everyone except the scrum-halves, the scrum off-side line runs through the tail-end of their side of the scrum. (Thus there are *two* off-side lines, one for each team.) Normally, when the scrum forms properly, the line runs through the feet of the number eight forward, since these stick out furthest. Until the scrum ends every player who is not part of the scrum must keep both feet behind this line. The scrum ends when the ball is heeled out, so the side which gets the ball starts off with anything up to ten or twelve feet of clear ground between it and the nearest tackler (except for the opposing scrum-half) – enough space to start an attack.

This, of course, is the purpose of the law. It rewards the side which has won possession with enough room to exploit it. It keeps the attacking potential of the half-backs in balance with the destructive abilities of the defending back row, an equilibrium which, not so long ago, was being seriously threatened by a breed of plundering flank-forwards who were being allowed to pillage and loot and generally turn half-back formations into devastated areas.

Figure 28 A flank-forward who leaves a scrum before the ball has been heeled out must immediately move straight back behind the off-side line, and stay behind that line until the ball comes out. He can break back like this only if he is behind the ball at the time

Flank-forwards must now *either* stay in the scrum *or*, if they want to leave it, get back behind their off-side line. And they can leave it only if they are behind the ball. This means that in a 3–4–1 formation, where the ball has reached the second row, the flank-forwards on that side must not break *at all* until the ball has come out. They are in front of the ball, and so they cannot leave the scrum. When they are *not* in front of the ball and they want to pull out, they must do it quickly, and not hang around to see what develops.

This, strangely enough, is something that many flank-forwards find hard to do. Sensing that their opponents are about to heel the ball, they disengage the binding arm and rise in dismay. Then, not being daft, they observe that the ball has not yet come out, so there is no point in charging forward in pursuit of it, at least not yet. On the other hand they hesitate to rejoin the scrum in case it *does* come out. And so they hover, torn by indecision, the brow clouded, the lip gnawed, the entire body about five feet off-side.

Hamlet would have made a lousy flank-forward. Today's player has to make a snap decision and act on it. Either stick to the scrum until the ball comes out, or beat it back behind your off-side line. But don't dither. A dithering flank-forward stands out like a grandmother in the Grenadier Guards. Not many referees could miss one of *those*.

Any flank-forward who pulls out of the scrum before the ball has come out is obviously reducing his side's shove. If their opponents start marching the scrum up the field, he may wish that he were back with the boys, fighting the good fight. In fact there is nothing to stop him rejoining the scrum, as long as he does so behind the ball.

When we were talking about heeling the ball, we said the number eight forward could detach himself from the scrum and pick up the ball, he being on-side because by his departure the tail-end of the scrum moves up a row (assuming they're packing 3–4–1). This should be crystal-clear now that we've covered the scrum off-side law too. We said that the flank-forward could also pick up the ball if he found it coming out of the scrum in front of him. But if the flank-forward breaks from the scrum and, before he can get back behind the off-side line, the ball emerges in front of him, he must not touch it; he's still off-side. The law is very simple: any forward who decides to leave a scrum before the ball has come out must first and immediately put himself on-side by retiring behind the off-side line. All other business can wait.

When the scrum turns . . . ?

Uncouth players who think they can make the referee look a bit of a goon will sometimes stare at him over their beer and ask, nastily, 'What about when the scrum starts turning, then?' And they wait while he shuffles his feet and mumbles that he doesn't really know about when the scrum starts turning, and he wishes someone would tell him.

So do we all.

The problem is this. The scrum off-side lines work like a charm as long as the scrum is pointing north and south, up and down the field. But suppose it starts to rotate. Suppose it turns until it's pointing east and west. Where are the off-side lines then?

Presumably they are still running through the tail-ends, only now the sides are the ends, and the tail-ends are probably the flank-forwards' elbows. The two off-side lines are now divided by the width, rather than the length, of the scrum, and God knows where the scrum-halves can safely put themselves.

But suppose the scrum keeps *on* turning, until it has gone through a semi-circle, and instead of pointing north and south it's pointing south and north. Where are the off-side lines then? The tail-end of each pack of forwards has merged into one line, running through the middle of the tunnel – and if a flank-forward were to break, he would have to run *forwards* to put himself on-side. Meanwhile, the opposing backlines have been able to advance with their respective off-side lines, until now they are eyeball-to-eyeball. A hideous prospect. God forbid that anyone should heel the ball. The only player who could legally go and get it would be the opposing scrum-half.

The thing has happened, of course, many times in many games; and as soon as the scrum has turned through more than ninety degrees it has become impossible to disentangle the various overlapping off-side lines. There is only one solution, as far as I know, and that is for the referee to give the scrum a hefty biff on the nearest corner and hope that it will keep on spinning until it ends up where it began.

Wheeling the scrum

A spinning scrum is just an act of God, whereas *wheeling the scrum* is a shrewd tactical move, about which the laws know all.

You don't see much scrum-wheeling these days, and this is a pity, because it's a dashing manoeuvre which, rightly executed, can cleave a cleft through the enemy ranks compared with which the Parting of the Red Sea was like opening a garden gate. It works like this.

Blacks are playing Reds. Blacks hook the ball and hold it in their second row. Suddenly, the entire Black pack shifts its weight so as to make the scrum wheel. When it has turned enough – say fifty or sixty degrees – the Black second row wrenches itself free *against* the direction of the wheel, thus lurching into the open space left where their opponents used to be, and charges forward with the ball at its feet and the back row thundering along behind in support.

Done properly, it's a move that is usually good for about thirty yards and a couple of nervous breakdowns.

Looked at narrowly, of course, the second-row forwards have broken from the scrum without retiring behind their off-side line and you might say that this was wrong. You would get no support from the laws. Players wheeling a scrum can leave it without the usual restrictions, so the laws say, and a good thing too.

2 Rucks

If you have thoroughly read and completely understood all the preceding guff about set scrums – all right, don't lie to me – you won't have any trouble understanding rucks.

A ruck is simply a scrum with all the starch taken out of it. Its purpose is the same – to get the ball back in play – and most of the laws that cover a scrum apply to a ruck.

The big difference, of course, is that you can't have any specialists in a ruck, which is simply a first up, first down affair. This cuts out all the scrum-half/hooker/flank-forward/number eight rubbish, because none of those gents is recognizable in a ruck. And we are spared the pomp and ceremony of Putting The Ball In, since the ball is already in. This effectively eliminates any special scrum-half off-side law, because after all *any* player could be scrum-half at a ruck, so no favoured treatment is going to be handed out there. There is only one off-side law for rucks, and it applies to everybody.

What is a ruck?
First things first, however. What exactly is a ruck? It's important to know this, because you are not, for instance, allowed to handle the ball in a ruck. On the other hand, if you hesitate to grab the thing because you aren't sure whether or not a ruck is taking place, you could be missing a slice of glory. So pay close attention.

To have a ruck, all you need is one player from each side in the field-of-play, on their feet and shoving each other, with the ball on the ground between them. If any other player joins the ruck, he must bind on to a team-mate; but the heart of a ruck is simply a pair of opponents, shoving over the ball on the ground. If they are not opponents, or if they're not shoving each other, or if the ball is not on the ground, or if it's on the ground but not between them, then it's not a ruck, and you can go where you like and do what you will (subject to the other laws, of course).

Off-side at a ruck
The ruck off-side lines run through the tail-ends of the ruck, just as they do in the set scrums. If you are not in a

Figure 29 This get-together meets all the requirements of a ruck – ball on the ground and opponents over it shoving each other. The off-side lines run through the tail-ends of a ruck. You must either join it (from your own side) or get behind it

ruck you have a choice. You can either get behind the ball and then join the ruck, or you can get behind the ruck. If you decide to join it, you must bind on behind the ball. Otherwise, you must stay behind the off-side line until the ruck is over, which is when the ball comes out.

Rucks tend to take place unexpectedly, of course. It is not uncommon for a whole slew of players to be caught off-side when a ruck suddenly breaks out. Nor will they suffer for it, necessarily. Provided they don't hang around, and provided they do their little best to scurry back where they belong, the referee will look upon them charitably. It is when he sees them shambling back, and notes that they are not displaying that bustle and vigour of ten minutes ago when they thought they were going to score a try for the first time in twelve years; it is when he sees them bloody well *mooching* around the ruck on all sides like a lot of fat bridesmaids jockeying for the garter; it is when he sees them glancing coyly at their off-side line and deciding that, 'No, no, really they couldn't, it's just too too far' – *that* is when he gets impatient and starts handing out penalty kicks.

When you come to think of it, there is precious little point in ruck-mooching and risking getting caught for being off-side. If you're going to get stuck into a ruck, you might as well pull your finger out and *do* it. If you're not, then you might as well prepare to make yourself useful when the ball comes out. If it comes out on your side, you'd better be behind it, for obvious reasons. It *might* come out on *their* side, of course. On the other hand, it might not. If it doesn't, and you are still hanging about off-side, you'll be perfectly positioned to do sweet nothing. Can this be good?

There are various other things to say about rucks – things like don't handle the ball in a ruck; don't do anything to make the ruck collapse, such as falling or kneeling, or jumping on top of other players; don't – if you're lying on the ground – interfere with the ball or miss any chance to roll away from it; don't bring the ball back into a ruck . . . but you know all that stuff by now anyway.

In any case, it's all common sense. As we said before, a scrum is to heel the ball away. You can't have people deliberately preventing either the scrum or the heel from taking place – and that applies to rucks too. Much scoring comes after rucks (we used to call it 'a quick heel from the loose' and now the okay phrase is 'second-phase play', but it adds up to the same thing) so every player should understand them. That means backs as well as forwards. There is no class discrimination at the bottom of the heap.

3 Mauls

The big difference between a ruck and a maul is that for a ruck the ball must be on the ground, whereas for a maul the ball must be carried. *A ruck needs only two players, whereas a maul must have at least three: one from each side around the man who is carrying the ball, in the field-of-play, and all of 'them wrestling for possession.* You are not in a maul unless you're caught up in the struggle or bound on to it. A maul ends a tackle.

Figure 30 A maul is like a ruck except that the ball is held, not on the ground. The off-side lines run through the tail-ends just the same, and you must either join it (from your own side) or get behind it

Maul off-side

The off-side law for mauls follows the same lines as scrum and ruck off-side. The off-side lines for a maul run through the tail-ends of the maul. And – just as in a ruck – you have a choice: you can *either* get behind the ball and join the maul, *or* get behind the maul and stay there until the maul ends, which is when the ball comes out.

Maul-mooching has about as much future as ruck-mooching, i.e. none.

Five Touch, and the line-out

Touch

Where is it? Touch is the area beyond the sides of the field-of-play, and I'm not going to attempt to define it more than that.

Three things save touch from being a complete waste of time. One, it provides somewhere for spectators to stand. Two, it gives the players somewhere to throw their orange peel at half-time. And three, it marks a definite boundary to the field-of-play, without which everybody would be on the point of collapse after about four minutes.

Once the ball goes into touch it becomes dead, and play is re-started by throwing the ball in. The touch-line is in touch, but the corner-posts are not – they are in touch-in-goal, which is a different story.

The ball alone. If the ball is in free flight (not held by a player) and it touches or crosses the touch-line, then it is immediately in touch. This means that even if the ball crosses a touch-line and is blown back so that it pitches in the field-of-play, it has still gone into touch. When the ball is on its own, the touchlines are considered to extend vertically and for ever, and any invasion of airspace beyond those lines counts as going into touch.

There is one exception to this. If a player, who is himself in the field-of-play, manages to reach over and catch the ball as it's coming down on the other side of the touch-line, then it is not in touch. But this is true only if the ball crossed the touch-line just before he caught it.

The ball carried. When a player has the ball, the vertical barrier is down and touch is a more horizontal thing. If the ball, or any part of the player carrying the ball, touches the touch-line or the ground beyond it, the ball is in touch.

Notice that the player must be *carrying* the ball, and one or other of them must *touch* the ground, before the ball is in touch. If the player carrying the ball lets it swing out over the touch-line, it is not in touch. If he is not carrying the ball and he ends up in touch while the ball is still in the field-of-play, he is allowed to kick it. He can even, if he wants to, knock it backwards with his hand, as long as he doesn't hold it.

Remember that the actual touch-line is in touch. If you have the ball and you so much as prod the chalk with your toe, then you're in touch, and the ball with you.

The line-out

The line-out, like the scrum, is simply a way of getting the ball back into play, quickly and fairly. Unlike the scrum, however, where you must have two front rows before you can put the ball in, it is not essential to have a formed line-out before you throw the ball in: see *Quick Throw-in*. But if you don't take a quick throw-in, then you must form a line-out, and there are certain guidelines about that.

Usually, and especially towards the end of the second half, when the knees are buckling and hot flashes streak across the eyeballs, your average line-out begins to look like a Naafi queue during the siege of Sevastopol.

All the faults which the players have been trying to avoid suddenly take over.

The line-out *should* be formed opposite the place where the touch-judge is signalling – but the players shamble up to a nearby spot and hope that the touch-judge will move over to them. The front of the line-out *should* be at least five yards from the touch-line – it ain't; it's four, or three. The two lines *should* be straight and parallel to the goal-

Figure 31 Two views of a line-out – one all wrong, the other rather better. A line-out should have two single, straight, parallel lines, with a clear gap of two feet between the lines, and with each player standing at least a yard from the next man of his team. Both lines should start at least five yards from touch, at right angles to the place signalled by the touch-judge

lines – but one line is pure switchback, and the other points right at the corner flag. There *should* be a clear space two feet wide down the middle – but it's clogged with bodies. The team-mates in each line *should* be standing at least one yard apart – but some are leaning on each other like sets of unemployed book-ends.

This is not the ideal way to re-start the game.

The ideal line-out is a very simple thing. It is two straight lines, two feet apart, formed by players who are at least a yard apart from their team-mates. The front of the line-out is at least five yards from touch opposite the mark signalled by the touch-judge, and the back is no more than fifteen yards from touch.

The man who throws the ball in is an opponent of the side which last touched the ball when it went out. (And it makes no difference if they didn't mean to touch it, or if they were reluctantly forced into touch while holding the ball – they still lose it. Deciding who throws the ball in is simply a matter of deciding who last touched it, and giving it to the other side.)

The player throwing in – usually the winger or the hooker – must stand in touch and throw the ball so that it goes at least five yards at right angles to the touch-line before it touches a player or the ground.

Now, the laws say that he has to throw the ball *straight* along the line-of-touch, which is an imaginary line running through the touch-judge and across the field, parallel to the goal-lines. (So it follows that the line-out forms up on either side of the line-of-touch.) The purpose of a line-out is to re-start play quickly *and fairly*. Both sides must be given a reasonable chance of getting the ball, and if there's a small gale blowing from left to right, it's obvious that a short, hard throw stands a better chance of landing in the right place than a long, soft one.

If the player throwing in makes a hash of it – stands in the wrong place, or doesn't throw it five yards, or doesn't throw it in straight – the other side can choose either to take the throw-in themselves or to have a scrum fifteen yards in. If they decide to have a second throw-in and they too get it wrong, then the referee orders a scrum.

So. As the wing stands poised to lob the ball, picture the scene: two single, straight and parallel lines, starting five yards in and separated by a healthy respect for the invisible line-of-touch. Bear all that in mind while we have a bash at the next bit, which affects so much of the line-out that we might as well do it now: the dreaded (but really simple) *line-out off-side*.

Line-out off-side

'People,' Marx * once observed, 'come in two sorts. There's the workers, who do the grafting; and there's the rest, who get the benefit.'

He was talking, of course, about the line-out, which is divided for the purposes of off-side into:

1 those taking part
2 all others

Those taking part are all the players involved in throwing the ball in, catching it, and disposing of it. In chronological order they are the man with the ball (and his opposite number), all the forwards standing in the line-out, and the one player of each team in position to receive the ball from the line-out – usually (but not necessarily) the scrum-halves.

Those not taking part are all the others – the backs (stand-offs, centres, wings, full-backs) and any forwards who have chosen not to join the line-out.

Off-side for those taking part in the line-out

Until the ball is thrown in, the off-side line for those taking part is the line-of-touch. No player must put a foot across this imaginary line, unless he's jumping for the ball; and if he jumps and misses he must hustle back without delay.

As soon as the ball is thrown in and it has touched a player

* Dr Henry Marx, perhaps Rutland's heaviest-ever line-out forward.

or the ground, the off-side line runs through the ball itself. Every player in the line-out must stay on his own side of the ball until the line-out is over. (And if you don't know when that is, don't worry, we'll get to it later.)

So off-side for players taking part in a line-out is quite straightforward. Until the ball is thrown in, keep behind the line-of-touch; after that, keep behind the ball.

Figure 32 *Illegal!* The line-out off-side line runs down the middle until the ball is thrown in; then it runs through the ball. Either way, the nearest Black player has gone too far. In his desire to cream the scrum-half he has got himself well off-side

Off-side for those not taking part in the line-out

The off-side line for players *not* taking part is even simpler. It's a line ten yards behind the line-of-touch (which is like saying ten yards behind the line-out) and parallel to the goal-lines – or the goal-line itself, if that happens to be nearer. And as before, all players *not* taking part in the line-out

Figure 33 The off-side line for players not taking part in the line-out (normally only the backs) lies ten yards behind the line-out. Until it ends, all players not in the line-out must stay behind this line. The only exceptions are the scrum-half, who can stand between the two, and one opponent who can mark his opposite number throwing in the ball

must keep both feet behind their off-side line until the line-out is over. (In the case of the goal-line they can keep both feet *on* the line, since the line is in the in-goal.)

If you have this situation clearly imprinted on what for want of a better word we may call the mind, you will see that it creates an area up to twenty yards wide between the opposing back-lines. Whichever side wins the ball from the line-out is rewarded with a healthy acreage of sod in which to start hatching its devilish plots before the foe can pour across no-man's-land and start registering vigorous protests.

This is what the law is for. There is no point in winning the ball if you get a tackle like a Turkish earthquake immediately after it. Once the line-out is over the forwards can set off and do their worst, but it has been proved repeatedly that the ball can travel faster than the man. (Ask any forward.) What's more, the forwards are limited by the *length* (in distance) of the line-out. This is tied up with when the line-out begins and ends, so we had better have a stab at that.

The length of the line-out

The side which is throwing in the ball sets the length of the line-out by the position of its furthest player in the line-out.

I shall say that again, backwards.

Wherever the furthest player of the side throwing in the ball decides to stand, that is the limit of the line-out. He is the last man, and anybody else who stands beyond him (and not ten yards back) is off-side. It may sound unfair, but it's one of the perks of throwing the ball in. If the side throwing in decide they want a short line-out, their opponents have no option but to shorten *their* line, too.

But in any case, no line-out player is allowed to stand more than fifteen yards from the touch-line. As the front of the line-out must be at least five yards from touch, this means that the actual line of players can never be more than ten yards long.

When the line-out begins

The penny drops at the moment when the ball leaves the hands of the player throwing it in. At that instant, the length of his team's line marks the limits of that particular line-out for good and all. If the furthest man then steps forward, his opponents needn't keep pace with him in order to stay on-side. On the other hand no player – from either side – can go beyond the back-marker until the line-out is over. (Except in the case of a *long throw-in* over the tail of the line-out – but that's not really a line-out at all. We get to long throw-ins a bit later.)

Even when the ball has left the hands of the player throwing it in, that doesn't give the line-out men a free hand. They must keep that two-foot-wide space between the lines unless they're actually jumping for the ball. And they must stay at least a yard away from their nearest team-mate until the ball has touched a player or the ground unless they're either jumping for the ball or peeling off. This strikes me as a pretty broad exception, because everyone in the line-out *can* jump for the ball, if they want to, just as anybody in the line-out can peel off, if he feels like it. But according to law, those one-yard gaps between players and that two-foot space between the lines should survive until the ball has touched someone or something.

When the line-out ends

The line-out ends when one of four things happens:

1 The ball leaves the line-out.
2 A player with the ball leaves the line-out.
3 The ball is thrown beyond the last man in the line-out.
4 A ruck or maul has formed, and the *whole* of the ruck or maul moves beyond the line-of-touch.

When any one of those things has happened, the line-out is over and line-out off-side is a thing of the past. In the case of the first three, the ball is in open play and anyone can go anywhere (subject to the usual off-side law). In the case of the fourth – where a ruck or maul has formed – the off-side law for rucks or mauls applies (obviously). So the back-lines can immediately move up to the tail-ends of the ruck or maul.

Notice that the line-out comes to an end, not when a ruck or maul forms, but when that ruck or maul has completely moved away from the line-of-touch (that's the imaginary line running through the middle of the line-out).

A ruck or maul in a line-out is still a line-out, and so the back-lines must stay ten yards behind it.

When the ruck or maul gives a convulsive shudder and lurches clear of the line-out – all of it, not just most of it – then the line-out has ended and the ruck/maul is promoted to Grade A status, with its own off-side lines, luncheon vouchers, pension schemes, and so on. And *that* is the moment when the back-line can, without fear of savage reprisals, nip smartly forward. It pays to know just when you can make that move without risking a penalty kick between your uprights. That's why I'm telling you all this.

Where the ball-thrower can go. Also the scrum-half
While all this crucial decision-making is going on, what of the man who threw the ball in? He has done his bit – thrown it to number three in the line-out, Big Bert, only Bert wasn't quite ready so the other side caught it – and now he's watching rather anxiously, wondering what he can do to help.

After he has thrown in the ball there are only four things which the thrower (and his opposite number) can do, legally, until the line-out's over:

1 Stay where he is, between the line-out and the touch-line.
2 Get stuck into the line-out.
3 Nip round the side and play scrum-half, provided the bloke who normally plays scrum-half is ten yards back.
4 Get ten yards back himself.

If he sees a gap in the line-out, he can flit into it and take the ball, or rather he could if he hadn't just thrown it. Certainly his opposite number, and either of the scrum-halves, can exploit any gap they see in front of them, as long as they don't go barging into players as they do it.

Peeling-off
The lawbook, you will recall, goes to some lengths to spell out who is in the line-out and who is not. And it goes to

Figure 34 Peeling-off at a line-out is okay – provided you don't start too soon or run too deep. You must not peel off until the ball has left the thrower's hands, and then you must keep close to the line-out, or you'll be off-side

considerable lengths – up to ten yards – to separate the two. Naturally, having done this, it wants to keep up the good work until the line-out is over. If you are ten yards back, you must not wander forward. If you are in the line-out, you must not stray back. Only one man can stand between the line-out and the back-line, and he is the scrum-half.

On the other hand, once the ball has been thrown in you can't expect the forwards to stand at parade rest while they watch who catches it. They want to do their little bit to help, and that often means unplugging themselves from the line at spot A in order to get stuck in again at spot B. That, as the actress said to the bishop, is only human nature.

The laws, in their boundless wisdom, allow this. That is to say, they don't forbid it. (The laws allow everything which they don't forbid.) But at the same time, they keep a tight grip on players who are peeling-off.

For a start, you must not begin to peel off until the ball has left the thrower's hands. Then, you must keep close to the line of the line-out *and* you must keep moving until either you get stuck into a ruck or maul, or the line-out ends.

How close is 'close'? How long is a broken bootlace? Look at it this way: at a line-out the scrum-half is a privileged player, because he's allowed to stand between the line-out and his back-line. Each team is allotted one scrum-half, and you can't increase that number by having spare forwards falling back from the line. If the referee sees a forward in the slot reserved for the scrum-half, he's more likely to think that he is sloping off than that he's peeling off.

How close is 'close'? Nobody knows. But a good rule-of-thumb whenever you're peeling off is to be where you can reach out and touch the line-out. Anywhere deeper than that is a bit dodgy, especially if you're taking a pass or knock-back.

Line-out off-side round-up

Here, then, is a quick wrap-up of the various ways you can be off-side at a line-out.

Off-side at the front of the line-out. The line-out begins five yards from touch. If you stand nearer to touch than that, you are off-side (except the relevant throwers-in).

Stepping out of line. Each line of forwards must leave a clear space down the middle until the ball is thrown in.

If you step into this space, you're off-side.

Overstepping the ball. Once the ball has been thrown in, the off-side line runs through the ball. If you get in front of it, you're off-side.

Penalty. These three cases of line-out off-side all involve players who are taking part in the line-out, so the penalty kick is awarded on the line-of-touch, fifteen yards in from touch.

Off-side at the back of the line-out. The furthest player in a line-out must not be more than fifteen yards from touch, or he will be off-side. Subject to this maximum, the length of the line-out is set by the side throwing the ball in. If you are on the other side, and you stand deeper than your opponents' last man when the ball leaves the thrower's hands, you are off-side. Furthermore, if you move beyond this backmarker's position before the line-out has ended, you are off-side (except in the case of a long throw-in).

Peeling-off too soon or too deep. If you peel off before the ball has been thrown in, or if you peel off and run too far from the line-out, you are off-side.

Not ten yards back. If you're not taking part in the line-out you must stay ten yards behind it. If you don't get back far enough, or if you advance too soon, you're off-side.

Penalty. In these three cases of line-out off-side, the offending players are reckoned to be *outside* the line-out, and so the penalty kick is given on their off-side line (i.e. ten yards back), opposite where the offence took place. This mark must be at least fifteen yards in from touch.

I fancy I hear ugly mutterings from the back of the hall. Evidently there are those who feel that Rugby, far from being the simple sport I promised, has developed into something bloody diabolical, so can they have their money back?

Stick with it, lads. Rugby *is* a simple game, even including line-out off-side.

The thing about the line-out is that whilst there are no

end of complicated ways of getting *off*-side, there is only one, very simple way to stay *on*-side. Master that, and you're home and dry.

The line-out has a simple shape. It starts here and it stops there, and between these ends are two straight, single lines. Stay in line until the ball arrives, and keep behind the ball until the line-out ends, and you won't go far wrong.

You can always find trouble if you go looking for it; but in that case don't blame the laws for making life difficult. It's really your option.

Keeping what's left of your nose clean
There are a couple of other things which the laws would rather you didn't do in a line-out. Most of them can be summed up in these two commandments:

1 Until the ball is thrown in, don't touch anyone.
2 After the ball is thrown in, don't touch an opponent unless he has the ball, or unless a ruck or maul has formed.

Barging in the line-out. If there is a clear space down the middle you shouldn't be touching an opponent. Most barging takes place when players are jumping for the ball and one player is more concerned with putting his shoulder into his opponent than getting his hands on the ball. This is illegal, and can even be dangerous: a player jumping at full stretch is very vulnerable to a bash in the ribs. Fortunately, a barger in the line-out stands out like a docker in a chorus line, so the referee invariably nobbles him before he can do much harm.

Ankle-tapping the jumper. As your opponents' master-jumper launches himself into space, it may occur to you to stay down at ground level and wait for his feet to come up to you, and then violently remove them, with the result that he has nothing to land on but the back of his head. After all, why not?

Because the laws forbid it, is why not. Feet-pulling or ankle-tapping of a player jumping in a line-out has been ruled *prima facie* dangerous play. *Prima facie* is Italian for 'Take that innocent look off your face'. (It's all right, they play Rugby too.)

Using another player as a prop. The human-pyramid act has obvious attractions in a line-out, and if the laws didn't forbid it God only knows where the whole thing might end. As it is, the only assistance you're allowed in jumping for the ball is from your own puny legs.

Holding and obstructing. You've seen it; I've seen it; we've

Figure 35 *Illegal!* The laws forbid any player to help another to jump for the ball in a line-out by holding him up

all seen it, and not a few of us have done it. The ball is thrown in, it bounces about, someone taps it back and it lands on the deck. The scrum-half goes after it, the opposing forwards *try* to go after it, and a wall of arms holds them back. This is obstruction. You must not hold or push or

Figure 36 *Illegal!* In any part of the game it is illegal to obstruct an opponent who hasn't got the ball – and that goes for line-outs, too

deliberately obstruct an opponent who hasn't got the ball. The urge to protect your winnings is strong. It is tempting to fling out an arm and hold your opponent back, and it is easy, and it is illegal.

This is true of all parts of the game, of course. It's just that obstruction seems more natural in a line-out. Players who wouldn't think of grabbing an opponent to keep him from tackling someone in open play will feel that they are being quite noble by holding off an opponent who has designs on their scrum-half.

There is, I suppose, a bit of a difference. A line-out by its very nature presents a wall of brawn between one lot of forwards and their opponents' scrum-half, and the brawn has every right to arrange itself in such a way that nobody can get through. But what it hasn't got a right to do is to grab, barge, or deliberately obstruct any opponent who would otherwise have got through. You're entitled to *be* in his way but not to *get* in his way.

The too-short throw-in. The short throw-in to the front man in the line-out is a thing you see fairly often, and if players knew how dangerous it was they would turn grey. Pseudo-scientific research has shown that as often as nine times out of ten, the ball doesn't travel the minimum of five yards.

When this is the result of general lassitude and tired blood on the part of the gent throwing it in, the referee is authorized to pension him off and let the other side have a bash. But when it's caused by the greed, impetuosity and ape-like reach of the man who caught it, the laws take a much dimmer view. The only penalty laid down for deliberately preventing the ball from being thrown five yards is a penalty kick. Even if you're standing five yards in, you must also be sure to let the ball come to you – not reach forward and go to it.

I once knew a seven-foot-tall wing-threequarter and a six-foot-five forward who practised all summer until they could stand five yards apart and hand the ball to each other. It was beautiful to see. Convinced that they had a match-winning tactic, they introduced it during the first line-out of the opening match. When the referee gave the other side a penalty, one of them had a nervous breakdown and the other slipped a disc, and they never played again. Sad, really, because the forward had quite a good voice. Baritone.

Figure 37 *Illegal!* At a line-out the thrower must throw the ball in five yards – and nobody must stop it going five yards. This throw-in is too short; the penalty is a penalty kick

Rare and unusual line-outs

Not every line-out has all the stirring pageantry and solemn ritual described above. Some are short, scarcely as long as they are wide. Some are full-length, yet never see the ball. Others are non-existent, but the ball is still delivered impeccably. All are perfectly legal.

Short line-out. The minimum number of players in a line-out is two from each side, and if the side throwing the ball in decides that a two-man line is a good idea, their opponents have no choice but to go along with them.

If, however, the side throwing in already *has* eight men in the line-out, they cannot decide then to pull six of them out and leave two; it's too late for that. The decision must be made *before* these players formed up in the line-out. Once they're in they must stay there until the line-out's over.

This is to save time. At one point in the development of the game, line-out forwards were departing one by one and two by two on both sides, until the original sixteen were whittled down to four, and the scrum-halves couldn't see their stand-offs for refugee forwards, all standing around worrying about what they would do if someone gave them the ball here, now, in all this open space. That kind of nerve warfare is now out.

Opponents of the side throwing the ball in are given a bit of leeway, though. Since they don't know how many men the other side is going to put into its line, they've got to prepare for the worst. Then, if it turns out to be a short line, the referee will give them a reasonable amount of time to withdraw the extra players before the ball is thrown in.

For instance, if Blues kick the ball into touch a yard from Whites' goal-line, and get ready for an orthodox, eight-man line-out, Whites might decide to form a short, two-man line and hold the other six in readiness in their in-goal. In that case, Blues would be given time to pull out six of *their* forwards, before Whites went ahead and threw the ball in.

Long throw-in. The invisible line-of-touch stretches – in theory – right across the field, and if you've got a man who can throw it that far there's nothing to stop him hurling the ball right past the line-out and into the wide open spaces – as long as it pitches on the line-of-touch.

As soon as the ball leaves his hands, any player in the

line-out or out of it – forward, scrum-half or back – can run out to catch this long throw-in. The backs can run forward, and the forwards or scrum-half can run beyond the backmarker. But if they anticipate a long throw-in which doesn't then take place – if the ball does not in fact clear the backmarker – they're off-side.

Now let's take this a stage further. Suppose the side throwing in decides to have a mini-line-out (which can be as small as two men from each team, remember). What's to stop them putting one man at the front of the line and the other man at the back, so that they're ten yards apart? Answer: nothing, except perhaps bitter experience.

Here is the situation. The side throwing in certainly has the right to decide the length of the line-out, and provided their men are at least a yard apart they can bunch up, or spread out, or do a bit of both. However, if the backmarker isn't *reasonably* close to the next player in his team – and that's a relative term, depending on how the other players are spaced – then the laws say he's not in the line-out. That makes him off-side (so he's not really the backmarker at all) except for one interesting loop-hole. If the ball is thrown directly to him, everything's okay – provided, as always, that it's thrown in straight.

If some of you are beginning to suspect that I may be obsessed with throwing in straight, you can relax, because I am.

Throwing in straight is the crucial part of the line-out. All the business of long throw-ins, and deep-standing backmarkers, and so on, depends entirely on the accuracy of the thrower. And any discussion of the legal niceties is so much wasted breath when the player throwing the ball in has an effective range of about fifteen yards, and that only on days of flat calm. Show me a long throw-in where the ball has travelled more than twenty yards, and I'll show you a seven-to-four chance that it didn't go straight. Seven-to-four? Make it eight-to-three.

Quick throw-in (no line-out at all). All it takes to throw the ball in from touch is the ball and someone to throw it. A line-out is an optional extra.

Suppose a long kick sends the ball into touch at the other end of the field. Nobody is there except the full-back and the touch-judge, who signals where the ball should be thrown in. The full-back gets the ball. The nearest player is

Figure 38 Quick throw-in. A line-out is not essential to re-start play. As long as you do it properly you can take a quick throw-in without waiting for a line-out

still forty yards off, and closing slowly. Why wait? The full-back throws the ball in, making sure that:

1 he stands at the right place,
2 the ball goes at least five yards, and
3 you guessed it – the ball goes in straight.

He then hurries across, picks it up, and belts it or runs with it or does whatever Part II of his plan calls for.

So you don't have to wait for the line-out to form before you throw the ball in. As long as you use the same ball that went into touch, and only the players have handled it (no help from the audience, for obvious reasons), you can take a quick throw-in, either by throwing the ball to a team-mate or by just throwing it.

Some players may be off-side, but that doesn't matter. As long as they're trying to get back for the line-out, they won't be penalized.

Where is the line-out held?

Rugby is basically a game of handling and running. Okay, there are moments when you have no choice but to bang the ball into touch, but the laws discourage unlimited touch-kicking.

It boils down to this. Outside your own 25, if you kick directly into touch – that is, if the ball doesn't land in the field-of-play before it goes out – then your kick gains no ground for your side: the ball is thrown in opposite the place where you kicked, not at the place where it went out. Inside your own 25, you may kick directly into touch and still gain ground.

The only exception to this is penalty kicks. From anywhere on the field, a penalty kick straight into touch results in the ball being thrown in where it went out. Just be careful not to kick the ball twice. Some players have got

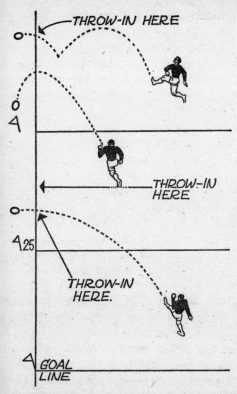

Figure 39 Outside the player's 25, direct touch-kicking does not gain ground. Penalty kicks are an exception

into the habit of taking quick penalties by tapping the ball with their foot, taking a pace forward and kicking for touch. The first tap is actually the penalty kick, and the kick for touch is an ordinary punt.

A free kick (kick from a fair catch, or 'Mark!') is *not* an exception. If, however, you make a mark outside your 25, you can retire inside the 25 and kick directly to touch. A small point, but worth remembering.

If, from outside your 25, you kick directly into touch and actually find touch behind you, then that's where the ball is thrown in, not opposite where you kicked. You get the worst of the deal, whatever it is. And if, from a kick-off, you kick the ball directly into touch, your opponents can (if they wish) take a line-out opposite the place where you kicked, i.e. on the half-way line.

Naturally, any touch-kick which bounces in the field-of-play, or any grub-kick which goes into touch, gains ground for the kicker's side. The ball is thrown in where it crossed the touch-line. And that applies if the ball touches an opponent, too. It's a direct kick to touch only if the ball touches nothing at all on its way.

Touch-judges. There are two of these officials, one for each touch-line, and their job is to help the referee by following play up and down and signalling (with a small flag provided for the purpose) whenever the ball goes into touch, or touch-in-goal. In the case of a high kick, this may involve some fast geometrical calculation in the old think-tank: what matters is where the ball crosses the line, not where it comes to earth.

The touch-judge also signals which side is entitled to throw the ball in, so he has to decide who last touched the ball. If the kick was made outside the kicker's 25, the touch-judge has to decide whether or not it went directly into touch, and locate the throw-in accordingly – sometimes with the referee's help.

It's important that the touch-judge should flourish his flag the very moment the ball goes into touch. Often the referee is watching for this signal because, what with all the dust and steam, he can't actually see the ball.

Next, the touch-judge should stand at the appropriate spot, still keeping his flag up so that everyone can see him, and point to whichever side is to throw the ball in. Having done this, he should keep on doing it and above all *stay where he is* until the ball has been thrown in. If the players line up in the wrong place, the touch-judge should hold his ground, perhaps flaring the nostrils a little. What he should not do is feebly shuffle sideways. Just because they have it wrong, there's no need for him to get it wrong, too.

If the wrong team throws the ball in, or if the man who throws it in steps in the field-of-play, the touch-judge should keep his flag up as a signal to the referee. On the other hand, the referee can overrule him and let play go on – for instance, if advantage applies.

The touch-judges also help the referee when kicks at goal are being taken – penalty kicks, free kicks, or conversions. (For penalty kicks or free kicks, where the kicker can decide whether or not to go for goal, the referee usually signals the touch-judges to come round behind the posts, using a sweeping gesture rather like a druid loosening up before a big sunrise.) One touch-judge stands at or behind each goal post; if the ball goes over the bar he raises his flag. If the ball goes directly over the top of the post he doesn't raise his flag. The posts, like the touch-line, are considered to soar heavenwards indefinitely. If the ball went over one it must have hit it.

You might think that this is a lot of needless fuss about a rather dreary part of the game, and you would be completely wrong. Anyone who has played in a game where one touch-judge was eleven and always gave the ball to the home team because his big brother was playing on that wing, and the other touch-judge was eighty-three and never got closer than forty yards to the action all afternoon, knows that good touch-judging is worth having.

It's the responsibility of the team captains to produce touch-judges, and the traditional arrangement is for the teams to provide one each. Or so it should be. In a great many clubs, the tradition is to forget all about it until the referee asks, and then shout vaguely in the direction of the crowd of drinkers outside the clubhouse. The results are usually disastrous, but that doesn't stop the players complaining bitterly about unfair or inaccurate decisions. But then, nothing will.

Six The law that nobody knows

Off-side and on-side following a quick ruck,
maul or line-out

Nobody knows? I exaggerate. At the last count, four people
did actually know this law: two referees, a sportswriter who
has since left the country, and me.

You may remember that, back in the Middle Ages, we
said that in open play – not during scrums, rucks, mauls or
line-outs – you could be off-side only if you were in front
of someone on your team who had the ball, or who last
played it. That is what we said and we make no apology for
it, because it's true – 99·9 per cent of the time.

There is just one situation, however, in which it ain't
true. You can be off-side, *even though your opponents have the
ball and no scrum, ruck, maul or line-out is taking place*, if
they have just forced a snap scrum, ruck, maul or line-out
between you and your line, won the ball and started an
attacking movement. In that situation you are off-side and
there's nothing you can legally do until they have put you
on-side, which they can do only by kicking the ball or
running five yards with it. Passing the ball does *not* put you
on-side, not after they've forced a snap action and won
quick possession from it. Understand?

No. As I thought. From the rows of sagging jaws, glassy
eyeballs, and calloused thumbs scratching numbed skulls, I
can see that we have achieved something less than total,
blinding comprehension. Perhaps we should try it again,
this time more slowly, playing on both the black and the
white keys.

Picture this. Blues are playing Whites, and all the action is inside the Blue 25. Suddenly, a Blue player breaks clear and puts in a tremendous kick ahead. The Blue team races upfield and catches the White full-back in possession. A maul forms. Blues win the ball, get it out and start an attacking movement. *See* Figure 40, a, b and c.

At this point some White defenders arrive on the scene, pounding back to help save the day. Obviously they *were* off-side during the quick maul, but the maul is over now. On the other hand, would it be fair to let them rush into the game and destroy the Blue attack? An attack which the Blue players sweated for and earned by being faster and more quick-thinking than Whites?

Wouldn't it be like rewarding Whites for being slower, and might it not be an incentive against hurrying back to join the maul (or scrum, or line-out), or at least to get behind it where they're on-side? After all, if the leisurely

Figure 40a Blue player breaks away in his own half and puts a long kick deep into the White half

Figure 40b White full-back catches ball as Blue players zero in.
White defence is slow getting back

QUICK
POSSESSION
FROM RUCK.

OFF-SIDE

Figure 40c Blues ruck and quickly win the ball. As they start to
attack, White defenders arrive but are off-side

defender can turn up and straight away tackle an attacker, he might deliberately take his time, reckoning that Blues are going to win the ball anyway, and he can do more damage if he catches them starting an attack and tackles from behind than if he hurries and gets in front, where they can see him.

Clearly, slow play cannot be allowed to succeed at the expense of fast play. So the sluggish defender is made to pay for being late. An off-side defender who is retiring towards a scrum, ruck, maul or line-out is, of course, covered by the appropriate off-side law while the scrum, ruck, maul or line-out is going on. But then, if his opponents have won the ball and he's still slogging back, he's covered by the Forgotten Law of off-side, which says that he must not interfere with play until he's been put on-side.

And only his opponents can do this. There is no off-side line for him to retire behind. The only way he can become on-side is for an opponent to kick the ball, or run five yards with it. Until then, the defender can only wait and curse, and he'd better do *that* under his breath.

In general play, a player is always put on-side the moment an opponent plays the ball, e.g. passes it. But this is not general play; it's a sort of untidy aftermath; and the leaden defenders don't get let off so easily. They must concede their opponents at least a run of five yards or a kick before they can interfere. A pass alone is not enough to put them on-side; nor is two passes, or three, or four. Only a kick or a five-yard run will do the trick.

The situation outlined above (Blues v. Whites) doesn't often happen. There isn't usually such a great difference in speed and stamina between the attacking and the defending sides. But there is one aspect of the modern game where this particular off-side law does increasingly apply, and that's the quick heel from a ruck following a scrum or line-out.

Say that Blues heel from a scrum and the ball reaches

Figure 41a From a scrum, Blue stand-off gains fifteen yards and is tackled. Blue back row breaks fast and zeroes in

Figure 41b Blues ruck, quickly win the ball and start an attack. White back row finally arrives on scene from 'Blue' side, but is off-side

their fly-half, who gains fifteen yards and is tackled. Immediately, the Blue back row zeroes in and rucks for the ball. They heel it out and are ready to start another passing movement when the White forwards arrive on the scene, too late to ruck but eager to tackle – and all off-side. *See* Figure 41a and b.

Now, the ruck is an important part of the game. When a team can't penetrate the defence with an attack from a set piece, it may deliberately force a ruck and start a second attack while the defence is disorganized.

Knowing this, a couple of the defending forwards may decide to take their time about covering across the field after a set piece, on the principle that the best time to reach a ruck is just after your opponents have heeled from it. Which is true as far as it goes. It just doesn't take into account the basic nature of the game. Rugby is meant to be a fast-moving, attacking game, and the Forgotten Law of off-side exists to protect that aim. It is very seldom applied, but it's always there, if needed.

Seven Scoring

The aim of the game is to score tries.

Naturally, any team which takes the field without at least one man who can kick penalty goals from all parts of the field-of-play and adjoining counties is being unnecessarily kind to its opponents, but still – the aim of the game is to score tries. A try can bring you a maximum of six points, whereas any other score is worth only three. The moral is obvious.

Try

You score a try by being the first to ground the ball in your opponents' in-goal, and this is worth four points. You don't have to carry the ball across the line: you can chase someone else's kick or pass, and fall on it, or you can kick it ahead yourself and follow up and score. In fact the only thing you must be sure of is *grounding the ball* – which is not necessarily the same as touching it down, or touching it when it's on the ground. For instance, picking up the ball in the in-goal is not grounding it (so you can pick it up and run towards the posts if you want to improve the chances of conversion).

Grounding the ball
You can ground the ball in one of three ways. If you are holding it you can simply touch it to the ground. Some people think that it's necessary to press down, but it's not. They are thinking of the second method: if the ball is

already on the ground, you must press down on it with your hands or arms (one is enough). Alternatively, if the ball is already on the ground you can fall on it so that it's under your body anywhere from the waist to the neck. Note that in this way you don't have to lay a finger on the ball. You can ground a ball, and score a try, simply by diving on top of it and hitting it with your shoulder, chest or stomach – provided you get there first.

On the other hand, if you *are* holding the ball, make

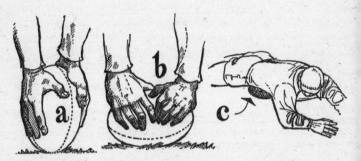

Figure 42 Three ways of grounding the ball: (a) hold it and touch the ground with it; (b) press down on it when it's on the ground; (c) fall on it so that it's under you anywhere between waist and neck

quite sure that the referee has seen you touch it down. Occasionally you will see a player race fifty yards, swerving out of seven or eight tackles, beat the full-back with almost contemptuous ease, stroll over the line between the posts, and deposit the ball without so much as breaking stride. The sad thing is that he hasn't actually *touched the ball down*: he got within an inch or two of the turf and then gracefully let go, like a goose demonstrating the laying of a golden egg. And if the referee was paying close attention, then he won't have blown for a try.

It pays to let everyone see that you have actually grounded the ball; and any player who is so pleased with his brilliant approach work that he neglects this finishing touch is asking for trouble. It's not that the referee is being bloody-minded; it's just that he has no alternative. He can't say to himself, 'Stone me, that feller deserves a try after a run like that, even though he didn't really score one,' can he? He must do what the laws say.

Personally, if I had galloped fifty yards with the ball – well, let's be realistic: if I had lumbered ten yards with the ball and gone over the goal-line, I would slam it down good and hard. And if I didn't hear the whistle I'd keep leaning on the ball until either the referee blew or I woke up and realized I'd only crossed the enemy 25.

Where are the lines?

The goal-line is part of the in-goal, so you can score a try by grounding the ball on the goal-line. The goal posts are also part of the in-goal, and if you have grounded the ball so that it is touching your opponents' goal post, you've scored. Whether or not the referee will agree with you is another matter, and there is no doubt that it's safer to get the ball right inside the in-goal.

The touch-in-goal lines and the dead-ball line are not in the in-goal, so you can't score on them. The corner flag, since we're picking so many nits, is part of touch-in-goal, but the flag – the actual cloth – is not; it's nowhere; it doesn't exist, in law.

Pushover try

A scrum can score a try. If one side shoves so hard that they push their opponents back over their goal-line and then ground the ball, it's a try. The cardinal sin of handling in the scrum doesn't apply, for the glaringly obvious reason that there ain't no scrum once it has crossed the goal-line; a scrum can take place only in the field-of-play. If the *defenders* ground the ball after a pushover, it's considered a touch-down and leads to a five-yard scrum.

Sliding over to score

If you get tackled when you're hurtling for the line, but your hurtle is so momentous that it carries you over and you ground the ball, that is a try, even if the ball has already touched the field-of-play on the way. It's all a question of momentum. Your thrust has to be so irresistible that it carries you into the in-goal. If the tackle stops you short of the line, you must not try and wriggle over, or stretch out and score. You're tackled, so the only thing to do is let go of the ball.

Scoring from touch

If the ball is in the enemy's in-goal and you are in touch or touch-in-goal, you can fall on it and score. If you pick it up, of course, you're an idiot.

Penalty try

If a defender does something unfair or illegal which, in the referee's opinion, prevents a *probable* try, then he will award a penalty try. The interesting word here is 'probable'. The referee doesn't have to be absolutely convinced that a try would inevitably have been scored; he just has to feel sure that the attacking side had a healthily odds-on chance. With that in mind, he can award a penalty try for an offence in mid-field just as much as for one inside the defenders' 25. A penalty try is always given between the posts. Contrary to popular myth, the defenders *can* charge the kick at goal.

Converting a try

Scoring a try gives a team the right to attempt to convert it into a goal (that's why it's called a 'try') by taking a kick at goal. A conversion is worth a further two points. The kick is taken exactly in front of the spot where the try was scored: anywhere on a line through the place of score, parallel with the touch-line. If the try was scored between the posts, it's a short, easy kick from right in front. If the try was scored in the corner, it's a long, hard kick from near touch. The kick can be a place-kick or a drop-kick.

Anyone on the scoring side may take the kick, and he can have a placer to hold the ball if he wants. All the rest of his team must get behind the ball, and all their opponents

Figure 43 Kick at goal after a try (conversion kick). Defenders must stay behind the goal-line until the kicker starts his run-up. Then they can charge, wave or jump – but not shout

must be behind the goal-line until the kicker begins his run-up or offers to kick. They can then charge or jump and try to deflect the ball, but even if they touch it and it goes over the bar, the goal is good.

What they must not do is shout as they charge. If they do, or if they offend in any other way – charge too soon, for instance – the referee can allow the same kicker to take a second kick without any charge. If, despite the defenders' wrongdoing, the first kick goes over, then the referee lets it stand and chalks up two points to the forces of righteousness.

Should any of the kicker's team be crazy enough to be in front of the ball when kicked, the kick is void. The same applies if the kicker uses a placer – hardly anybody does nowadays, unless it's blowing a gale – and he kicks the ball out of the placer's hands before it has touched the ground. The placer must place, you see. I once knew a placer who used to hold the ball on his right toecap, which (I now know) is all wrong; but the kicker never got anything over anyway, so nobody paid much attention.

Get on with it

The laws make it clear that all kicks, including conversions, must be taken without delay. That means the kicker must not be 'unreasonably slow', and if you want to know how slow is unreasonable, it's whatever the referee thinks. Most referees seem to think that a minute should be enough to take a kick at goal, starting from the moment when they awarded the kick – which, for a conversion means when the try was scored. You'd think a minute was plenty of time to tee up the ball and give it a blind boot, and so it is. The trouble is that many teams are so stunned by success that they leave the ball lying and forget all about the kick. By the time they've got hold of a kicker, and he has got hold of the ball, the first minute has about eight seconds left. That, of course, is entirely their fault; and if the referee were to disallow the kick and proceed at once to the centre of the field, they might wake up next time. No side has a right to waste its opponents' time.

Indeed, even if the kicker takes a full minute to bring off a kick at goal, no more than forty seconds of playing time will be lost, because the referee will simply add on the extra kicking time at the end of that half of the match, just as he already adds on any injury time. This applies whether or not he considers that the kicker has taken unnecessarily long over his kick. A kick at goal can take more than forty seconds, but it can never use up more than forty seconds of playing time.

If you think that all this stopwatching is a bit superfluous, it isn't. There is a good reason for keeping a tight rein on these delays. Kicks at goal can easily total fifteen or even twenty minutes, which means up to one quarter of playing time. Check out a few games for yourself if you don't believe me.

It's not essential to waste any time at all after you've scored a try, of course. The conversion attempt is optional; you needn't take it if you don't want to. This has happened – usually right at the end of a game when the scoring side needed more than two points to win, and preferred to use the remaining time in an attempt to score another try. It has been known to succeed, too.

Penalty goal; goal from a free kick

Strictly speaking, a goal in Rugby is a converted try, worth a total of six points. You can also score a dropped goal, a goal from a penalty kick, and a goal from a free kick. Each is worth three points.

A penalty goal or a goal from a free kick must be either a place kick or a drop-kick in the field-of-play, and of course the ball has to go over the opponents' cross-bar. (You can read all about penalty kicks and free kicks in the section on Kicks.) A penalty kicker can place the ball on the ground, but a player who is taking a free kick at goal must – unless it's a drop-kick – use a placer to hold the ball for him; if the kicker handles it when it's on the ground, the kick is void. Even if the referee orders 'no charge' and allows a second kick, the man who is taking a free kick must not handle the ball on the ground. But the ball must touch the ground before it is kicked; as with conversion attempts, any free kick at goal that gets booted straight out of the placer's hands is void.

If the defending side misbehaves while the kick is being taken but the ball goes over just the same, the referee will

Figure 44 Penalty kick at goal. Defenders must stand still, with their arms by their sides, until the ball has been kicked

give a goal. If it doesn't go over, he can award a second kick without – if it's a free kick – any charge. And if he thinks that the ball would *probably* have gone over if a defender hadn't illegally got in its way, he can even award a goal without the ball crossing the bar at all.

The time limits for these kicks at goal are the same as those for conversion attempts: one minute is usually regarded as a reasonable maximum, and even so, everything over forty seconds is made up in the same half of the match.

Dropped goal

You can score a dropped goal (three points) any time the game is going on, except at a kick-off or drop-out. All you have to do is drop-kick the ball from the field-of-play over your opponents' cross-bar. Even if an opponent touches the ball (or *vice versa*) before it goes over, it is still a goal. This applies to all kicks at goal. But if you drop-kick for goal and the ball touches one of *your own* players before going over, it's no goal – not because he may have diverted it but because he must have been, at the very least, accidentally off-side.

A dropped goal need not be the slick, well-oiled action you normally associate with international half-backs. All that is required is a drop-kick that sneaks over the bar; and a drop-kick is simply a ball that has been dropped and kicked after the first bounce. If you get tackled in the enemy 25, drop the ball in a blind panic, lash out and kick it on the first bounce, and accidentally send it flying between the posts, that's worth three points. Crummy points, but they all count.

Indeed, when you look closely at the definition of 'goal', it even seems possible to take a *place* kick at goal *at any time* during play (except the kick-off). You score a goal by *any* place kick from the field-of-play that goes over your opponents' cross-bar. In theory, then, the scrum-half could throw a long pass out to his stand-off, who could instantly place it for the waiting full-back to run up and kick for goal. It's all perfectly legal, and it might be a way of getting more length and accuracy than a drop-kick at goal would provide.

Anyway, that's what they believe in American football (a game that evolved from Rugby), where they take kicks like that all the time, and where I got the idea. I've never seen it done in Rugby, but it sounds as deserving of three points as any dropped goal.

Blown back; hitting the woodwork

If the ball goes over the cross-bar and the wind blows it back, a goal is scored. (This ruling was made in 1885, so blowing back probably happened for the first time in 1884. The winter of '84 was terribly windy, I remember.) If the ball hits a goal post, or both goal posts, or the cross-bar, or all three, and then goes over the bar, a goal is scored. If the ball goes directly over the top of a goal post it is not a goal; but you knew that already.

Eight Kicks

Kick-off

The game starts, and re-starts after half-time, with a place kick at the centre of the half-way line. After every score, too, play re-starts with a kick from the centre, but not always a place kick. After any kind of goal (converted try, penalty goal, goal from free kick, dropped goal) the kick-off is a place kick from the centre spot. After an unconverted try the kick-off is a drop-kick taken on or behind the centre spot.

Who kicks off? A toss-up before the match decides who kicks off. The winner can *either* choose which end he wants to defend *or* take the kick-off. If he prefers to choose ends, his opponents take the kick-off; if he wants the kick-off, his opponents choose ends.

Naturally, after half-time, when they change ends, the other side kicks off; and after a score it is always the side which has been scored against that kicks off.

What makes a good kick-off?
First, it must be in the right place: the centre of the half-way line for a place kick; on or just behind the centre for a drop-kick.

Second, it must be the right type of kick.

Third, the opposing team must stand at least ten yards from the half-way line.

Fourth, they must not charge until the ball has been kicked.

Failing any of these conditions – if the kicker makes the

wrong sort of kick, or the right kick in the wrong place; or if his opponents stand too near or charge too soon – the referee will order the kick to be taken again.

Fifth, the kicker's team must all be behind the ball. If the referee sees any of the kicker's team in front of the ball at the moment of kick-off, he will order a scrum at the centre.

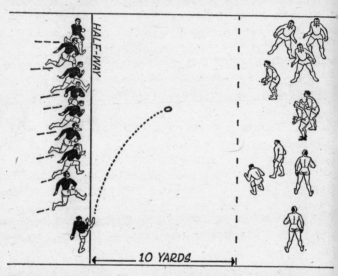

Figure 45 Kick-off from the centre. Kicker's team must be behind the ball when kicked, and opponents must be at least ten yards away. The ball should reach the ten-yard line and land in the field-of-play

Sixth, the ball must reach the ten-yards line (a line ten yards from the half-way line and parallel to it) unless an opponent plays it first, in which case the game goes on. If it doesn't go far enough, the opponents can either have it kicked off again or take a scrum at the centre. If it goes ten yards and the wind blows it back, play goes on.

Seventh, the ball must land in the field-of-play or the in-goal. If it is kicked too far, so that it pitches directly in touch or touch-in-goal, or even over the dead-ball line, the other side can choose to have it kicked off again, or take a scrum at the centre, or – if they like – accept the kick and all that goes with it, such as a nice line-out.

This all makes sense. The purpose of the kick-off is to start the game in such a way that both sides have a fair chance of getting to the ball and doing something with it. By making one team stand back, and making the other team kick the ball to them, the laws create a situation in which anything could happen, and usually does.

No advantage. There's not much in Rugby that is *not* covered by the advantage law, but the kick-off is one example. The game must start with the right kick from the right place.

Historical footnote. Devotees of worthless trivia might like to know why the kick-off after a goal is always a place kick, while after a try it is only a drop.

Until 1934 all kick-offs were place kicks. In that year, during an International match at Twickenham, there was a conversion attempt which the referee considered no good but which the gents working the scoreboard rather liked the look of. He had no way of signalling his decision, and of course the kick-off told them nothing, so they rang up two more points, which they later had to withdraw, of course, probably racked with humiliation, poor chaps.

So the sub-committee with special responsibility for kicks put its heads together and came up with this remarkably simple solution. The kick-off after an unconverted try is a drop-kick in order to keep the gents working the scoreboard from disgracing themselves. And if that doesn't win this week's Rugby Trivia prize, all I can say is there's no justice.

Drop-out

If the ball crosses a goal-line and is made dead there, play re-starts *either* with a five-yard scrum *or* with a drop-out, depending on several things which you can read all about in the section on 'In-goal'. A drop-out is a drop-kick by the defending side, taken anywhere on or behind their 25-yard line.

Figure 46 The 25 drop-out. The 25-yard line separates the kicker's team from its opponents. The drop-kick can be taken anywhere on or behind the line. The ball should cross the line and land in the field-of-play

At a drop-out, this line separates the two teams. All the kicker's team must be on their side of the line and behind the ball; all their opponents must be on the other side, until the kick is taken.

Up to this point, a drop-out is very like a kick-off: if the kicker makes the wrong sort of kick, or kicks from the wrong place, or if his opponents charge over the line too soon, the referee will whistle and order the kick to be taken again. And if any of the kicker's team is in front of the ball when it's kicked, the referee will order a scrum at the centre of the line.

Like the kick-off, a drop-out must go far enough but not too far. The ball must reach the 25-yard line; if it doesn't, the other team can either have the ball dropped out again or take a scrum at the centre of the line. (If the ball reaches the line and the wind blows it back, play goes on.) The ball should pitch inside the field-of-play. If it doesn't, the other side can either have another drop-out, or a scrum, or accept the kick (which means taking a line-out). All this, of course, follows the pattern of the kick-off.

Where a drop-out differs from a kick-off is in advantage. The advantage law applies to every part of the drop-out except the actual kick itself, which must be a drop-kick. For instance, if the ball doesn't reach the 25-yard line but an opponent gets to it first and gains an advantage, play can continue.

Penalty kick

1 *What the offending side must do.* A penalty kick is a kick given to one side because the other side has done something seriously wrong.

The side that has been penalized has to (a) hand over the ball, and (b) clear off quickly. Temporarily, the game becomes very one-sided. That is the penalty for doing things that are penalized with penalty kicks.

As soon as the referee has given your opponents a penalty kick, you must at once run – not walk, but run – to a line ten yards behind the mark for the kick, or to your own goal-line, whichever is the nearer. You can go further if you want to; but you must, if you can, give the other side at least ten yards of green grass in which to do their stuff.

Having given them the ball, the foreground and the initiative, you now have to give them your undivided attention, too. Until they have kicked the ball you must stand absolutely still with your hands by your sides. I don't know what you did to deserve all this, but let it be a lesson to you.

If you don't get back ten yards, or if you don't move

Figure 47 Part of the penalty of a penalty kick is that you have to give the other team a clear ten yards in which to do what they like with the ball. As soon as they're given the kick, you must *run* ten yards towards your own goal-line

fast enough, the referee will penalize you again by awarding a second penalty kick, ten yards in front of the first. (This second kick replaces the first.) And if you still hang around, he can move the kick up *another* ten yards. In fact, as long as you continue to fail to retire, he can continue to shunt you back, ten yards at a time, until the mark for the kick is only five yards from your goal-line.

That is the closest a penalty kick can be to the opponents' goal-line: five yards. When the offence takes place *less* than five yards from the line, the mark for the kick is always given on the five-yard line. This is to prevent the kind of situation where, with only inches separating the penalty kicker from the line, sheer brawn is bound to score.

Although the guilty team *must* retreat immediately, their opponents don't have to wait for them to do so. If they wish, they can take the penalty kick at once, even though both teams are still thoroughly mixed up – reckoning that the best time to attack is when the opposition is completely disorganized. And any opponent who is still within ten yards of the ball when this quick kick is taken will not be penalized, provided he is doing his best to get back.

Even so, he must then keep on retiring, *after* the kick has been taken, until he has covered ten yards or reached his goal-line. The taking of the penalty kick does not put everybody back into the game. There is a terrible temptation to stop and see what's going on, because after all they *are* the enemy, and they *are* up to something. Resist it. The first thing you must do is retire ten yards. Your opponents may be launching the most dangerous attack, but there's nothing you can do about it until you've put yourself back into the game by retiring ten yards – *with one exception*. If, while you are straining every nerve to retire ten yards, an opponent runs five yards with the ball, this brings you back into the game. You can stop retiring and get stuck in again.

There is a simple reason for this exception. Suppose that when your team is penalized, you are fifteen yards in front of the ball; that is, towards the enemy line. Your opponents take a quick penalty kick and start an attack. Now, you stand no chance at all of retiring ten yards behind the mark (making a total distance of twenty-five yards) and then rejoining the game, because play by then will have swept on and left you far behind. So the laws allow this second way out. As long as you're doing your best to get back ten yards, you can rejoin the game before you've covered the whole distance if an opponent runs five yards with the ball. Kicking or passing doesn't count: only a five-yard run.

2 *What the kicking side can do*. A penalty kick can be of any kind – place, drop or punt – and any player can take it. The kicker can use a placer to hold the ball, if he wants. The kick must be made either on or behind the mark, which the referee indicates with a delicate bash from his heel. Pay attention to that mark, and be sure you make your

Figure 48 Make sure you take the kick *through* the mark – not beside it or beyond it

kick somewhere on a line through it. If the referee makes his mark *here*, and you gallop up, all a-twitter with impatience, and take the kick *there*, two yards to the right, he'll make a rude noise with his whistle and give a scrum, opponents' ball.

You can take a penalty kick anywhere behind the mark, on a line through it and parallel with the touch-lines. This allows you to adjust the angle to improve your chances of a kick at goal. You can even go as far back as your own in-goal if you want to (I can't see what good it would do), but if you take the kick inside your in-goal you must kick the ball forward so that it crosses the goal-line before anyone on your team plays it again.

Apart from this, you can kick the ball in any direction, and any player – including the kicker – can play it next. Mind you, a penalty kick must be a *kick*. Bouncing the ball on your knee is not a kick. Tapping it on your toe is not a kick. A kick is only a kick if you hit the ball with your foot, or your leg below the knee, hard enough to send it out of your hands (if you're holding it) or away from the mark (if it's on the ground). It doesn't have to go far but it must go somewhere. More important, the referee must see that it has gone somewhere. If you turn your back on the referee and fumble with the ball, don't be surprised if he calls play back and orders a scrum; he's not clairvoyant, you know. Do the obvious thing: let him *watch* you taking the penalty kick. Then he can see that it is okay.

Once you've let the referee know that you're going to take a penalty kick at goal, you're committed to it. You must go for goal; if you try anything else the referee will disallow the kick and give a scrum. And there are more ways of letting the referee know than spitting on the ball and mumbling something about having a bash. If you start placing the ball as if for a kick at goal, squinting at the uprights, tossing little bits of grass into the wind, and so on, this says irrevocably that you are going for goal, and it's no good whispering huskily to him that really you're not. He may even ask you what you plan to do; he has the right.

The reason is simple. If you are taking a kick at goal, he will send the touch-judges around behind the posts. If you're not, he'll leave them where they are more use. What he *won't* stand for is sending the touch-judges behind the posts and then seeing you kick the ball into touch.

If you don't let the referee know that you intend to kick at goal, and then you take a drop-kick and it goes over, this is a goal. It just means that you've done it without benefit of touch-judges.

As with kick-offs and drop-outs and conversions, all the kicker's team (except the placer, if one is used) must be behind the ball when it's kicked. Otherwise the referee will give a scrum at the mark.

You are not obliged to accept a penalty kick, by the way.

You can have a scrum at the mark, if you'd rather. Up to you.

Drop-kick

You make a drop-kick by letting the ball fall to the ground from your hands and kicking it on the first rebound. The only times when you *must* drop-kick the ball are when making a drop-out and when attempting a dropped goal. Otherwise you might as well punt.

In the early days of the game, most kicks were drop-kicks. As late as the 1860s spectators booed punting; but the ball was a slightly different shape then. The oval leather case was filled with an inflated pig's bladder, and this usually made the ends well rounded. The ball was more suited to place-kicking and drop-kicking than today's relatively pointed ball, which is shaped for handling as well as kicking. Of course, a hundred years ago many people thought there was far too much handling in Rugby, too.

Free kick (kick from a fair-catch, or 'Mark!')

A free kick is not a penalty kick, and it has nothing to do with any offence or infringement. A free kick is a kick which a player earns by making a fair-catch, or 'Mark!'

Fair-catch. A fair-catch is a way of temporarily stopping the game. You must do three things, all at the same time:
1 *catch the ball cleanly* direct from an opponent's kick, knock-on or throw-forward.
2 *be standing still* when you catch it, with both feet on the ground,
3 *shout 'Mark!'*

This feat isn't easy, especially when the ball is coming out of the sun and the earth is trembling beneath the pounding hooves of hungry opponents. The usual time to make a fair-catch is when your team is in deep trouble and you need a break, so by definition you're under pressure. Nevertheless, you must bring off all three parts perfectly, and all together. If you catch the ball and then drop it, or if you don't have both feet on the ground, or if you complete (1) and (2) but shout the magic word one second afterwards – it's no good. The referee won't whistle up, and it's no use giving him that long, reproachful stare.

Figure 49 To claim a fair-catch, you must catch the ball, when you are standing still, with both feet on the ground, and bawl 'Mark!' – all at once

In fact, even when you've made a good fair-catch, you shouldn't hang around. Your opponents won't wait for the whistle, and neither should you. Beat it fast, while your legs still function. If the referee allows your fair-catch you haven't lost anything, and if he doesn't, then you're going to have to do something in a hurry anyway.

You can make a fair-catch in your own in-goal, and you can make one after the ball has bounced off a goal post or cross-bar. (You can also make a fair-catch from an opponent's knock-on or throw-forward *even though the referee has already blown for the infringement* – a little-known fact, and deservedly so.)

The free kick itself. The mark for a free kick is the mark made during the fair-catch. Only the player who made the fair-catch can take the free kick. He can take any kind of kick – place, drop or punt – and he can kick a goal. If he takes a place kick he must use a placer to hold the ball; he cannot place the ball himself. If the kicker handles the ball while it is on the ground the kick is immediately void, and the referee will order a scrum instead.

A free kick, like a penalty kick, can be taken at the mark or anywhere behind it on a line through the mark and parallel with the touch-lines. Unlike a penalty kick, a free kick can be charged: opponents can stand right up to the mark and charge a drop-kick or punt as soon as the kicker starts his run or offers to kick, and they can charge a place kick as soon as the ball touches the ground. This calls for good timing by the placer. If he puts the ball down too soon his opponents may charge the kick down; if he leaves it too late the kicker may kick the ball out of his hands, making the kick void.

The kicker cannot afford to waver or feint and then draw back. The moment he starts to kick his opponents will be after him, and if he hesitates they may succeed in blocking the kick altogether. Result: scrum.

This charge is the reason why most players take their free kick well back down the line through the mark: every step back widens the gap between the kicker and the chargers. But wherever you take the kick, you must kick the ball at least as far as a line through the mark, unless an opponent plays it before it gets that far. If you make your mark in the in-goal it is considered to have been made on the goal-line, so the ball must cross that line.

Inevitably, all the kicker's team (except a placer, if used) must be behind the ball when it's kicked. Otherwise: scrum.

Their opponents must keep both feet behind the mark. If they overstep the mark (source of metaphor) or charge too soon, or do anything childish like screaming, the referee will stop the game and give the kicker the option of a second kick without a charge. (The kicker might not accept this, if he has succeeded in putting away his kick and it's a good one, in which case advantage applies and the kick stands.) Any second kick must be taken by the same kicker, and all the old conditions apply, including no handling of the ball on the ground. However, the kicker can change the *type* of kick – for instance, from a punt ahead to a place kick at goal.

If the player who made the fair-catch is injured and can't take the free kick, the kick is void; nobody else can take it. Instead there's a scrum at the mark, with his team putting the ball in. And if he made his fair-catch in in-goal, the scrum goes down five yards out from the goal-line, opposite the mark.

Nine The in-goal

The in-goal is the area behind the goal-line. It is bordered by the goal-line, which is part of the in-goal, and the touch-in-goal and dead-ball lines, which aren't. So if the ball touches *them*, it is dead.

The great attraction of the in-goal is that it's the only place where you can score tries. Apart from that – and the fact that scrums, mauls and line-outs aren't held there – the in-goal is just like the field-of-play. A knock-on in an in-goal is still a knock-on; a player who is off-side in an in-goal can get into trouble just as easily as if he were in mid-field. Ninety-nine per cent of all the laws apply behind the goal-line just as they do in front of it.

But although the offences are much the same, the consequences are not. The referee's decision varies according to which side has broken the law.

If an attacking player breaks a law in his opponents' in-goal, the referee will order a touch-down, which means a drop-out.

For instance, if an attacking player follows a kick into his opponents' in-goal and knocks the ball on, the defending team get the benefit of his mistake.

(If his offence is a more serious one, the referee can also warn him or send him off. And if the referee decides that, if it hadn't been for this unfair play, the attacking side would probably not have scored a try, he can disallow the try and give the defending side a touch-down instead. Either way, the outcome is always a drop-out.)

If a defending player breaks a law inside his in-goal, the referee will order a five-yard scrum, attacking team's ball.

Before he stops the game he will wait a moment to see if

the attacking side can take advantage of the defending mistake, of course. If they don't, and if he decides that but for the offence the attackers would probably have scored a try, he can always award them a penalty try. (For instance, if a defender deliberately obstructs an attacker who is going for the ball in the in-goal.)

When the defender is guilty of foul play the referee can also warn him or send him off. But whatever happens, as long as the ball is in play, a defender's infringement in his own in-goal can result only in a five-yard scrum, or at the worst, a penalty try.

The in-goal and the penalty kick

A penalty kick cannot be awarded inside an in-goal. Nevertheless, there are two offences inside an in-goal for which the referee can award a penalty kick. The difference is that the penalty kick is taken on the field-of-play, not in the in-goal.

The first of these two in-goal offences is misconduct while the ball is out of play. Once the ball has gone dead, any kind of dirty work in an in-goal – I leave the grubby details to your steaming imagination – results in a penalty kick. This kick is taken at the place where the ball would next have been brought into play. For instance, if the misconduct followed a touch-down, the kick would be taken on the 25-yard line; and if it was a defender who committed the misconduct, the attacking side would be given the kick. And very likely put it over.

The second in-goal offence is deliberately obstructing an opponent who has just kicked the ball. The defending team can take either a penalty kick at the spot where the ball lands or a drop-out from their 25, whichever they prefer.

Ball goes dead in the in-goal

If a defending player carries or sends the ball over his own goal-line, and any player makes it dead there, the referee will order a scrum five yards from the goal-line, opposite the place where the ball went into the in-goal, and the attacking team will put the ball in.

If an attacking player carries or sends the ball over his opponents' goal-line, and *any* player makes it dead there, the referee will order a drop-out. The same applies if the ball unavoidably touches a defender before it crosses the goal-line: as long as he didn't try to play the ball and someone makes it dead, the referee will give a drop-out.

Note that it doesn't matter which side makes the ball dead. The important thing is who made it cross the goal-line in the first place. If a defender takes or sends the ball over his own goal-line, the laws feel that he must be responsible for the consequences, and if the ball goes dead they give his opponents a five-yard scrum. Even if a defender with the ball is *forced over* his line and touches down, it's still a five-yard scrum. Suppose a defender puts the ball over his goal-line and an over-eager attacker accidentally kicks it across the dead-ball line; the result is still a five-yard scrum. Whereas if an attacking player is responsible for putting the ball into the in-goal and either side makes it dead there, the defending side automatically get a drop-out. The same applies if an attacker knocks-on in the field-of-play so that the ball crosses the goal-line and is made dead: the result is a drop-out.

Kick charged down in the in-goal

It's not unusual for a defending team to carry or send the ball into their in-goal, and for a defender to try to kick it clear. And sometimes it happens that an energetic attacker charges down this kick. If the ball is then made dead behind the goal-line, play re-starts with a five-yard scrum, attacking team's ball. And it makes no difference if the actual charge-down happened in the field-of-play instead of the in-goal: it's still a five-yard scrum.

What 'made dead' means

For the purposes of this law, the ball is made dead behind

a goal-line when a defender touches it down, or when it goes on or over the touch-in-goal or dead-ball lines; with these exceptions: two ways of making the ball dead behind the goal-line which this law doesn't cover. They are:

1 when a try is scored, which of course leads to a kick at goal;
2 when a defender *in the field-of-play* deliberately knocks or throws the ball into touch-in-goal or over his own dead-ball line, which is illegal and gives away a penalty kick. (But strangely enough, if you do the same thing *inside your in-goal*, it's all right.)

Note that if a scrum is shoved over a goal-line and a defender grounds the ball in the in-goal, the referee will order a five-yard scrum. Until 1974 the decision in this case was a drop-out, but then the law was changed for the sake of consistency: after all, the retreating half of the scrum took the ball into their own in-goal (even if they didn't particularly want to), so they must pay for it.

What happens when the ball is held up in the in-goal?
If any player – defender or attacker – has the ball in an in-goal, and his opponents have got such a grip of him that he can't ground it, the referee will order a five-yard scrum, with the attacking side to put the ball in. The decision is the same whether an attacking or a defending player first put the ball over the goal-line. If the ball is held up in the in-goal, it's *always* a five-yard scrum, and it's *always* the attacking team's ball. Curiously, this five-yard scrum is formed opposite the place where the player was held up – which may not be the same as the place where the ball crossed the goal-line.

There can be no mauls in the in-goal, remember. This is one of the few laws which don't apply there. Another is the tackle, legally speaking. Tackles cannot happen in an in-goal, which is not to say that you can't grab an opponent who has the ball there. You can; but he won't be covered by the tackle law, so even if he cannot play the ball he is not bound to release it. And as there are no mauls, legally speaking, in the in-goal, other defenders can converge from all sides to help hold him up. Result: stalemate, which the referee breaks with his famous five-yard scrum.

Ten Advantage

The Advantage Law is the best law in the book, because it lets you ignore all the others for the good of the game. It goes like this.

When one side breaks a law, and the other side gains an advantage from this, the referee lets the game go on.

For example: if a player gives a forward pass but an opponent intercepts the ball and makes good use of it, the

Figure 50 An example of *tactical* advantage – where a player breaks a law and his opponents gain no ground but they get an opportunity to attack. White's forward pass is intercepted by a Striped player. His path is blocked by a second White player, but he can pass to the Striped player outside him, who is unmarked

referee will gladly forget about the forward pass. And the advantage gained doesn't have to be territorial; it can be tactical. Take the same example again: if the opponent who intercepted the forward pass found himself about to be tackled, he obviously couldn't hope to make much ground, so territorial advantage is out. On the other hand, he might have an unmarked team-mate outside him, just waiting to take a pass; in which case there would be a good chance of tactical advantage.

Now, perhaps, you see why people are always urging you to play to the whistle. It isn't just that the referee might have missed the knock-on (which you saw so clearly and slowed down because of). It's far more likely that he saw the knock-on *and waited to see if it gave any advantage to the other side.* For the referee, as we have discovered already, is not clairvoyant; the only way he can find out if you are smart enough to exploit your opponents' mistakes is by giving you the chance.

Therefore he must let play go on for a couple of seconds after the infringement, before he can decide whether or not an advantage has been gained. If you hesitate about grabbing an opportunity because you think the whistle *should* have gone, you defeat the whole purpose of the advantage law, which is to *keep the game going.* Let the referee look after the mistakes; your job is to get the ball and score. The referee will do all he can to leave these opportunities open to you, but only you can take advantage of them.

The advantage law covers ninety-nine per cent of the game. Virtually every time your opponents go wrong, you can profit from it. Advantage covers scrums, rucks, mauls, line-outs, knock-ons, forward passes, free kicks, penalty kicks, tackles, drop-outs, in-goal play, and all kinds and conditions of off-side. There are a million ways you can use advantage, and the referee will be looking for them all.

Exceptions. Only five parts of the game are *not* covered by advantage. They are:

1 The kick-off. This must be the right sort of kick, taken from the right place.
2 The drop-out. This must be a drop-kick.
3 When a free kick is void.
4 When the ball or a player carrying it touches the referee.
5 When the ball comes out of the tunnel at a scrum.

   Unless there's a penalty kick, it must be put in again.

   This last item raises an interesting point. The ball must be heeled properly; if it's not, if it gets booted out of the tunnel, advantage does not apply. But advantage certainly does apply to putting the ball *into* the scrum. If the scrum-half, in a fit of absentmindedness, puts the ball in crookedly under *the opposing* hooker's feet, the referee should let him get on with it.

Figure 51 An example of how advantage applies to an off-side situation. Whites, attacking near the Black goal-line, win the ball at a scrum. Black flank-forwards are caught off-side – but Whites might gain more by running the ball and perhaps scoring a try, than by kicking a penalty goal. So immediately penalizing Blacks for off-side is not necessarily to Whites' greatest advantage

The same thing applies to line-outs. The thrower is supposed to throw the ball in straight, but if his unstraight throw favours his opponents, why stop the game?

And if, at a drop-out, the ball goes backwards instead of forwards and the other side is waiting for it when it comes down, good luck to them. Also full advantage.

Consider a scrum near the posts. As the attacking side heels the ball the defending back row is caught off-side. Should the referee immediately blow up? Not necessarily. The attacking team might get a try and convert it: six points, against three for a penalty goal. So, while making it clear that he has seen the off-side offence, the referee can let the attack develop. If it fails, he can still award the penalty-kick for off-side.

One of the more irritating nuisances in Rugby is the player who keeps reminding the referee when something has gone wrong. He thinks he sees a knock-on, so he shouts 'Knock-on!'. This is stupid, because:

1 the referee, being human, resents being told what to do, and
2 he's playing advantage and trying *not* to stop the game, while this pessimist has never heard of advantage and spends his afternoon *looking* for reasons to stop the game.

The advantage law is a splendid idea. It makes playing a pleasure and refereeing an art. It is beautifully simple: when in doubt, play on! As Milton* once said, 'Advantage is the oil that greases the gears of the game,' and he should know. In Rugby, as in life, one man's grief is another man's gravy.

* Cedric MacGregor Milton, famed Manx referee.

Eleven Loose ends

What you can't wear
There's nothing in the book that says you must wear shorts
and socks and so on – you can turn out in velveteen breeches
and a moleskin waistcoat for all anyone can do about it –
but there are certain things you must not wear.

Dangerous lumps – things like belt-buckles, signet rings,
plaster casts – are illegal. This applies to the studs in your
boots, too, which must be of a certain size: no more than
$\frac{3}{4}$ inch long, for instance. (The full details are in the lawbook.)

Shoulder pads of any kind are illegal unless you've injured
a shoulder and the referee agrees that it needs some
protection. Even then, you can wear only soft padding,
such as cottonwool or sponge rubber, and the pad must not
be loose – it has to be either taped to your body or sewn to
your shirt.

There are absolutely no circumstances in which you are
allowed to wear shoulder pads of leather or any other hard
material. Nor can you wear a 'harness' type of shoulder pad.
If your shoulders are so frail and sensitive that they need to
be protected with armour, it's time you took up embroidery.

How long is a game?
International matches always last eighty minutes; so do most
county and top club matches. Below county level there is
usually no set time and the two teams can decide how long
they want to play. If they can't agree, the referee will make
the decision. There is no minimum time – seven-a-side

Rugby follows all the laws of the game and is played only seven minutes each way – but play must be split into halves, and at half-time the teams must change over. The half-time interval is five minutes at the most, and if both teams dislike standing about in the pouring rain they can scrub round the interval and kick off as soon as they've sucked their bits of orange; or sooner.

Injury time and other delays

If you are injured, you are allowed up to two minutes to recover. After that you must either get on or get off, always assuming that you *can* get off. If you can't, the referee will allow whatever time it takes to load you on to the stretcher. But for walking wounded, two minutes each is the maximum delay. This time is always made up in the half where it was lost.

Other delays which the referee may take into account are for things like lost balls, rabid dogs loose on the field, replacing the cross-bar (rare), re-erecting the goal posts (very rare), clothing the naked, searching for contact lenses, giving passage to livestock, and violent hailstorms (hen's-egg size and up). I remember a game where three minutes were added on for pushing the ambulance out of the mud. They couldn't leave it where it was: the bloke inside was bleeding all over the floor. Besides, the back wheels were right across the touch-in-goal-line.

What the referee will not allow delays for are things like broken or untied laces, thirst, legal discussion, tight boots, fatigue, blowing the nose, or getting yourself trapped upright in the scrum.

Leaving and entering the field

If you want to leave the field-of-play for any reason – even at half-time – you must get the referee's permission. Similarly, you must not come back until he allows it, which he will do only when the ball is dead.

When does the match end?
Unlike soccer – where, believe it or not, the final whistle can blow while the ball is in mid-air, *en route* from boot to goal – each half of a game of Rugby can end only when the ball is dead: for instance when the referee blows for an infringement. Even then, the game may not be over. If the referee has awarded a try, a penalty kick or a fair-catch, the kick is taken; and in the cases of a penalty kick or a free kick, play may well go on for some time longer before the ball becomes finally dead.

How many players? What about replacement?
You can have any number of players up to a maximum of fifteen in each team. Fifteen is the customary number, and seems about right for this sort of game; but if you can't raise that many, it's perfectly legal to play with less, as countless Sevens Tournaments have proved.

Substitution is not allowed in Rugby, with three exceptions. You can have replacements in recognized trial matches; these are purely internal affairs which don't really qualify as Rugby, since their purpose is to satisfy the selectors rather than the players.

Replacements are also allowed in certain other matches – for instance, those in which a national representative team is playing. Not more than two players in each team may be replaced, and then only for an injury which is so serious that an appointed doctor says the player should not continue playing.

The third exception is a special dispensation which allows Australia and New Zealand to practise the two-replacements-for-serious-injury rule at all levels of Rugby.

Rugby is a players' game, and clearly many players feel the need for a limited amount of replacement. Yet even here it's important to recognize that the person who benefits most is the spectator.

Well, spectators are very useful, and Unions make good use of their money. But international matches make up only a tiny fraction of all Rugby. In the vast majority of games, the player comes first by a long way; and replacement is not necessarily always in the players' interests.

To have substitution you must have substitutes – players who will probably not play, and who will certainly not play the full game. When a team has an injured player it may be handicapped, but when it exchanges that man for a fresh player its opponents may be handicapped even more.

And who is to decide when an injury is so serious that a man should leave the field? Only the player can tell. Only the player can know when he can or cannot go on playing. The trouble with substitution is that it inevitably affects his judgement, because instead of asking himself 'Can I go on?' he starts asking 'Should I go off?' The knowledge that the substitute is fit and fresh, while he is lame and weary, is bound to influence him, perhaps subconsciously.

Moreover, the examples of other sports stand as a grisly warning of what can happen when substitution becomes the rule. In soccer and in basketball the manager or the coach manipulates the games from the sidelines, switching players – or even entire teams – as he thinks fit. I have great respect for Rugby coaches, but I don't want to see them influencing the course of a match while it's actually taking place, thanks very much.

Rugby is a game between two teams who go out to play as well and as hard as they can until the match is over. For those seventy or eighty minutes the players are matched against each other; and who wins and who loses depends entirely on how each man plays. Nobody else can interfere, except the referee, and he is there more as an interpreter than a disciplinarian. Everything – all the decisions and the risks, all the effort and the struggle, all the success and all the failure – must come from those thirty men. That is the satisfaction of it: knowing when you go out that from now on it's up to you. No one who is not already on the field can help you or get in your way. This is a contest between these players, and only they will share the blame and the rewards.

Substitution obviously tampers with this idea. Well, Rugby has always shown a healthy ability to evolve and to adjust to new demands; and if enough players want more replacement no doubt it will come. But let nobody kid himself that the increase won't provoke new problems while it solves old ones.

Back in the early days of Rugby, they used to solve the whole problem by adopting what you might call 'reverse substitution'. Whenever an injured man had to go off, the captain of the *other* team sent one of his men off, too, thus restoring the balance and making it a true 'match' once more. There's a lot to be said for the idea – especially in seven-a-side Rugby, where any team that loses a player invariably loses the match as well.

What if the ball touches the referee?

1 *In the field-of-play.* If the ball – or a player carrying it – touches the referee in the field-of-play and neither side gains an advantage from this, he lets play go on. If he thinks one side *has* gained an advantage, he'll order a scrum on the spot. The team of the player who last had the ball will put it in.

2 *In the in-goal.* If the ball held by a player, or a player with the ball, touches the referee in an in-goal, he'll whistle up at once. If it was a defender who had the ball he'll award a touch-down; if it was an attacking player he'll award a try.

If the ball itself – not held by a player – touches the referee or a touch-judge or a spectator in an in-goal, the referee will whistle up at once and base his decision on what would probably have happened next. If he thought a defender would probably have got a touch-down or that the ball would otherwise have gone dead, he'll give a touch-down; if he thought an attacking player would probably have scored a try, he'll award a try.

If the ball touches a spectator in an in-goal and there is some doubt about what might have happened next, the referee will give the visiting team the benefit of his decision: a try if they are attacking, and a touch-down if they are defending. Maybe that'll teach the home side to keep their drunks locked up next time.

The end (nearly)

Congratulations. You have almost reached the finish of this gripping yarn, unless of course you are one of those people who always read the ending first so as to know how it all comes out. In which case I can tell you. In Rugby, everything always ends happily, because there is an Unwritten Law which says that following the battle you always buy your opposite number a pint. See you in the bar, then.

Index

Note: main entries are indicated in **bold** type